University of South Carolina

Report of the Chairman of the Faculty of the University of South Carolina

In Response to a Resolution of the House of Representatives and of the

Senate, passed February 18, 1875

University of South Carolina

Report of the Chairman of the Faculty of the University of South Carolina
In Response to a Resolution of the House of Representatives and of the Senate, passed February 18, 1875

ISBN/EAN: 9783337163013

Printed in Europe, USA, Canada, Australia, Japan

Cover: Foto ©Suzi / pixelio.de

More available books at **www.hansebooks.com**

REPORT

OF THE

CHAIRMAN OF THE FACULTY OF THE UNIVERSITY

OF

SOUTH CAROLINA,

IN RESPONSE TO

A Resolution of the House of Representatives and of the Senate,
Passed February 18, 1875.

COLUMBIA, S. C.:
REPUBLICAN PRINTING COMPANY.
1875.

REPORT.

RESOLUTION OF HOUSE OF REPRESENTATIVES, PASSED FEBRUARY 18, 1875.

Whereas the Superintendent of Education, in his annual report, presents the annual report of the Normal School, but neither the official report of the Chairman of the University nor a satisfactory report concerning the University itself; therefore, be it

Resolved by the House of Representatives, That the Chairman of the Faculty of the University be, and is hereby, requested to furnish to the House his annual report, with reports of the different Professors ; giving, besides such information as he may deem proper, the number on scholarships, their ages, the Counties from which they come, their general averages at the late semi-annual examinations, with the number and character of the studies pursued, and copies of the questions asked.

In response to the above request of the House of Representatives, I have the honor to present the following

REPORT:

COLUMBIA, S. C., February 19, 1875.

Hon. J. K. JILLSON, *Secretary of the Board of*
  Trustees of the University of South Carolina, Columbia, S. C.:

DEAR SIR—I have just received from the Clerk of the House of Representatives a request that I furnish to that honorable body my annual report as Chairman of the Faculty of the University of South Carolina, together with the reports from the different Professors. I placed my annual report in your hands, at the usual time last fall, for presentation to the Board of Trustees, and would now request of you a copy thereof, to present the same to the House of Representatives, in accordance with their request. I would ask of you, also, a copy of the report which I placed in your hands a year ago last November.

      B. B. BABBITT,
 Chairman of the Faculty of the University of South Carolina.

To this note I have received no reply in writing, and not till this report was all made up, on the 24th, did I receive a verbal notice that

I could have the reports on file copied. 1 have not the time to make the copy or the means to have the work done, and, therefore, would ask that your honorable body provide for bringing that report before yourselves.

In that report I endeavored to set forth fully the action of the Faculty, and their defense for that action, as criticised by the Superintendent of Education.

An examination of the two reports which the State Superintendent of Education has presented to the General Assembly shows that, during these two years, he has not presented to the Legislature either of these documents, or made any mention of them, while dealing himself specially with the very matter discussed in his reports.

It is true he promises in both reports, as Secretary of the Board of Trustees, a report from them, and calls the attention of the General Assembly to that forthcoming report; but no such report has as yet appeared during either year.

In his reports prior to 1873, at least in those of 1871 and 1873, he has given the General Assembly large and very "satisfactory" accounts of the condition of the University. (See the report of '71, and pages 14 and 71 to 73, in the report of '72.)

These, at all events, were "satisfactory" *at that time.*

But in the report for 1874 I find the following very severe criticism of the present status of the University :

" A sense of duty constrains me to make the following suggestions concerning the management of the University :

" 1. The adoption of a more strict and efficient system of discipline, and rigid enforcement of the same.

" 2. The elevation of the standard of admission in the University, and an unqualified adherence to the said standard.

" The practical operation of the Act to establish certain State scholarships in the University of South Carolina, approved February 20, 1874, has been, so far, a miserable farce. Under the provisions of said Act boys have been received into the University as State scholars who are not entitled, either by reason of poverty, merit or scholarly attainments, to receive the bounty provided by the State under the Act aforesaid. The end contemplated by the framers of the Scholarship Act was not to fill up the University halls with a motley crowd of youngsters, but 'that the advantages and benefits accruing from the State scholarships provided for in the first Section of this Act may be bestowed on suitable and deserving persons.' Your careful consideration of the forthcoming report of the Board of Trustees of the University of South Carolina is earnestly solicited."

This concluded a statistical statement, opened with an unofficial account of students in attendance on the University, both last year and the present year, in numbers far in excess of any figures reported for several years before.

I assume that this is accounted by your honorable body a report too meagre to be "satisfactory" and too severe in its criticism to be allowed to go forth unsustained or undisputed by official data. This must be apparent to your honorable body, in view of the most important events which happened in the history of the University during the past year, and of the more important bearings of those events on the cause of free schools, as well as in view of the deep interest which is felt in the question of impartial education throughout this country; for if the scholarship law has issued in a "miserable farce," the University, with its one hundred and fifty scholars, of every race and color, is a "miserable farce." Hence it is not surprising that your honorable body should characterize such a statement as not "satisfactory," coming, as it does, without one particle of evidence, except the stereotyped but annually unfulfilled promise of a "forthcoming report of the Board of Trustees."

These statements from the State Superintendent of Education cannot be true, unless the Faculty of the University have proved faithless to the high trusts committed to them, as the Board of State Examiners, under the scholarship law, and the higher trusts which they hold as the Professors and instructors in the University of the State. These statements ought not to be allowed to go forth throughout the country as the true accounts of the results of that most important experiment on which the University has entered, and through which it has struggled under great disadvantages during the past year and a half. Whatever may be the motive of this statement—and I have no desire to impugn the motive— the statement ought not to be given to the world except as the forced and unwilling confession of one compelled to make it after several years of trial, and I bespeak your most earnest attention, and I trust I shall have, also, your entire sympathy, in all honorable efforts for its refutation. Challenged, therefore, as I am, together with my fellow-workers, by your resolution to this refutation, I am happy to be able to present the accompanying statistics, in response to your request, and will add only a little more to what has been presented.

I will call the attention of your honorable body to the fact that the Superintendent of Education, as Chairman of the State Board of Examiners, must bear a portion of the responsibility of the execution of this scholarship law; yet I will testify, most willingly, to the fact that from the first he has consistently and persistently opposed the enforcement of the law—at first insisting that no students should be admitted last year to the benefit of the scholarships. He has always opposed the provisions whereby the Faculty would make it possible for students to come to the University, from outlying Counties. Against their efforts to bring the advantages of the University within the reach of those who from thence offered themselves for examination, he has always insisted that "the standard of admission into the University should be elevated and an unqualified adherence to its maintainence be required."

The Faculty have, in opposition to the State Superintendent of Education, followed out a middle course, providing a stepping-stone for those who otherwise could never have reached the lofty pedestal on which he would have us place the University, and yet they have kept the University itself intact, so that students, when they graduate, may stand with the best in the land. The Superintendent of Education has not visited the University to be present at any of its recitations, except at two of its classes, once each. He has not been present at a single examination, nor, so far as we know, has he reviewed the semi-annual examination questions, or the papers presented in reply. We do not say that, burdened as he is with the work of his office, he is, or should be expected, thus to visit our exercises, but we do claim that, not having the time to investigate, he has no right to condemn without investigation, much less, without giving the slightest reason for his condemnation.

With regard to the Superintendent's proposal to raise the standard of the University, I would make one remark. The honor of the University consists not so much in the exclusiveness of the standard as in the excellence and success of its instructions. If a "motley crowd" are admitted within its walls, and then a company of well trained students are sent forth ready for the work of life, in all its departments, the work of the University is successful. Whether we are doing this work can be now known only by personally visiting the University and inspecting its operations. The future alone can test this work fully. To the future, therefore, we must appeal to show the wisdom of our efforts.

In regard to the Superintendent's means of knowing what has been done in the assignment of the state scholarships, I will simply call attention to the fact that, excepting at the first few meetings, while we were determining the policy of the Board of Examiners, he has not been present at our deliberations, and so cannot know, of his own knowledge, the practical workings of the scholarship law.

With regard to the adoption of "a more strict and efficient system of discipline, and a rigid enforcement of the same," as insisted on by the Superintendent, I have to say that this has been the earnest desire of the Faculty, but, until lately, we have been hampered by the lack of laws, absolutely necessary to sustain the Faculty in the enforcement of discipline, and we are now still further hindered by the fact that we have not a copy of those by-laws, rules and regulations which we are required to put in the hands of every student, nor the means of printing them. In spite of these difficulties, I think that we may still say that what is necessary, in the particular of discipline, we shall have granted us in good time by the Board of Trustees.

The State Superintendent charges that "boys have been admitted into the University as State scholars who are not entitled, either by reason of poverty or merit or scholarly attainments, to receive the bounty provided by the State."

The accompanying schedule shows that the average ages of those admitted to State scholarships, (57 in number,) is:

For the Senior Class, 22 years;

For the Junior, 21.33;

For the Sophomore, 19.66;

For the Freshman, 18.53;

For the Sub-Freshman, 19—being the age necessary for graduation.

For the whole, the average age is 19.51.

In the Preparatory School, the average age of the scholars is, for the special students, usually called the "Shell Form," or, for the lowest form of all, 15.7; for the First Form, 13.76: Second Form, 17; Third Form, 17.

Total average, 15.5.

Thus, the average age of the Preparatory School would place them in the University. Less than one-third of the students in that school, or 24, are under the age required for entrance into the University, and 14 are 19 and over; that is, of sufficient age to be graduates of the University.

These are, certainly, not a "crowd of youngsters."

Accompanying this report is also a set of the examination papers on which the students were examined last October, when admitted.

Why, in his report, the Superintendent should have used the word "motley" in characterizing this "crowd of youngsters," whose entrance, he assumes, the General Assembly would deprecate, is not so plain. The dictionary defines motley as "variegated in color." The General Assembly, I maintain, meant the scholarships for all colors, and we have a goodly number of both white and colored students.

Motley means heterogeneous. I maintain that the General Assembly expected us to gather a heterogeneous crowd from all parts of the State. It could not well be otherwise. The results cannot be judged till it be discovered whether or not the motley crowd can be reduced to form, shape and congruity. What we have done you may learn by visiting the University and seeing for yourselves. There can be no grander sight to one who can see the principle involved than the gathering of this "motley crowd of youngsters," one hundred and forty in number, every morning at half-past eight o'clock for prayers.

The question of poverty raised by the Superintendent is wholly aside from the law. The record of the last session of the General Assembly shows that this condition of poverty, as necessary to the enjoyment of a scholarship, which was in the law when it was first framed, was cut out of it during its passage.

Finally, there has not been admitted a single student but he will at least comply with one of the requisites named by the Superintendent, "either poverty, or merit, or scholarly attainment." We do not claim infallibility, but it may be shown by the marks of the students, as herewith presented, that the number of mistakes in regard to their admission have been very few ; and that, considering the previous culture and training of these young men, their recent examination shows the results of their admission to the scholarships have been very far from a "miserable farce."

The attempt to break down the University and ruin the reputation of its Professors, since the changes which have been made in its method of administration a year or so ago, has come from so many sources, and such different directions, as to demand a thorough reply at the hands of the Faculty. I call your attention to the reports of the several Professors, herewith presented, with no little satisfaction and confidence that they themselves alone justify the action of the present Board of Trustees in their election, and show a most commendable degree of faithfulness in their labors as well as success in their efforts, and will satisfy your honorable body that the University was never engaged in a nobler, or a better or a more successful work than it is at present.

I shall take advantage of the permission given by your resolution, to give such information as I deem proper, to refer at this point to a recent attack upon those connected with the University by the Rev. Dr. Reynolds, lately of the Faculty, and to place on record some facts connected with the resignation of the late Dr. LaBorde. These facts are gravely misrepresented by Dr. Reynolds, in the memoir of Dr. LaBorde, placed as a preface to the recent revision of the history of South Carolina College.

Thus, on pages xv and xvi, we are told that the University would have equalled, if not surpassed, " the fame and usefulness of the College, but for the egregious folly and wickedness of those who held the control of the State." * * "A mixed school was impracticable. The colored people neither needed nor desired it." * * "But the Trustees were bent on a mixed school, and there were needy adventurers at hand to aid them in their attempts, * * who, even if unknown, or known only to be despised as incompetent or immoral, were yet subservient to their views." * * " The University thus became, both in its officers and its matriculates, a mixed school, and a policy which a Republican Congress has since refused to adopt, and so virtually repudiated, was allowed to effect the ruin of that seat of learning." It has " fallen into alien hands and sunk beneath contempt."

Professor Reynolds, in his memoir of Dr. LaBorde, undertakes also the task of making it appear that Dr. LaBorde shared in these feelings and opinions concerning us, which he has above expressed, and that he resigned because the University had become a mixed school, and to escape the contamination of a despised company of professors and students.

To allow such statements as these to pass unnoticed, when they may be used in corroboration of those made by the Superintendent of Education, would argue us culpably negligent of our own reputation and criminally careless of the reputation and success of the work committed to our care.

To show the falsity of such a view of his resignation, I place on per-manent record the following statement of facts :

At a meeting of the Board of Trustees, held during the first week of October, 1873, several members of the Faculty were invited to be present. They were requested to elect to the position of Chairman of the Faculty Professor M. LaBorde. Our unanimous reply was that we would only be too happy to acquiesce in the request.

On the following Monday, October 6, the Faculty met and elected him to that position. The Faculty was then composed of Professors Babbitt, Cummings, Fox, Gibbes, LaBorde, Lynch, Main, Melton, Roberts and Talley, as appears from their records. The next day, as appears from the register, Hon. Henry Hayne matriculated, and the record book was defaced. That afternoon a meeting was held, at which every Professor was present, except Professor Brewer, not yet arrived. Professor LaBorde presided as Chairman. The events of the morning were fully discussed, and it was the unanimous agreement of all the members of the Faculty that they would acquiesce in the situation, and be ready to enter on the work of educating all who, in accordance with law, were placed under our charge. On the next day, but one, October 9, a special meeting of the Faculty was called, at which were present the Chairman, Professor LaBorde, Professors Lynch, Babbitt, Cum-mings, Fox, Main and Roberts, the others having already resigned.

" The Chairman stated, in a very touching address, his purpose in calling the meeting to be entirely personal. In few words, he took leave of the Faculty, announcing that he had sent into the Board of Trustees his letter of resignation."

Thus stands the record. The Doctor, in broken accents, addressed us each in turn, and expressed his great regard and esteem for each, and his sorrow at the necessity which compelled him to leave a work on which he had hoped to have entered with renewed alacrity and zeal, but placed his final determination upon the fact that he had been assured that his position on the Faculty was not desired by those who were at the head of affairs, and that he was in the way of their plans for curtailing the scope of the operations of the University.

He unqualifiedly denied that he had resigned because he was unwilling himself to teach any who might come for instruction, but insisted that he was compelled to do so by pressure which he could not resist.

The Faculty appointed a Committee " to draft resolutions expressive of our personal regard for Professor LaBorde, in view of his statement to us." This being adopted, Professors Cummings and Babbitt were appointed to constitute that Committee. At the next meeting the following correspondence was read, and received as information :

COPY OF THE LETTER OF THE COMMITTEE APPOINTED BY THE FACULTY.

The undersigned, in behalf of the Faculty of the University of South Carolina, tender to Prof. M. LaBorde, M. D., this expression of the high personal esteem and sincere regret that, yielding to what he conceived to be his interest and duty, he has severed their ever pleasant relations as Professors in this venerable University. They trust that the eminent abilities and great moral worth which for so many years distinguished him in this institution, will, in new fields of labor, secure him friends and full measure of appreciation, and that his future days may be marked by usefulness and great happiness, and that, finally, his sun may set in a cloudless sky to rise in blissful immortality. In behalf of themselves and associates, they beg leave to remain his true personal friends and former fellow laborers,

A. W. CUMMINGS, } Committee.
B. B. BABBITT,

REPLY.

UNIVERSITY, October 13, 1873.

Rev. Messrs. CUMMINGS *and* BABBITT,

South Carolina University, Committee :

GENTLEMEN—Your note in behalf of the Faculty, tendering their high personal esteem for me, and their regret for the severance of our relations as Professors, has been received, and has given me very special pleasure. I will not disguise that I am ambitious of the good opinion of those with whom I have been associated, and shall ever remember with pride that though my connection with many of you was for a brief period, still it was long enough for me to earn your confidence and regard.

Most truly do I reciprocate the wish which you were kind enough to express for me, "that your" days for the future may be marked with usefulness and great happiness, and that when with us time shall terminate, you may enter upon a blissful immortality. Please convey my kindest regards to the other members of the Faculty, and accept for yourselves assurance of my personal regard and friendship.

(Signed)   M. LaBORDE.

It is plain that he whose last words were "I am at peace with God, and in perfect charity with the world," carried with him out of the University not the least particle of ill will towards his associates whom he left, and regretted nothing more than the necessity which compelled him to leave the work to which he was willing to give the end of his most useful life.

In the explanation of the reports of the several Professors, I would call attention to the fact that we have in the College courses proper besides the Sub-Freshman Class, the Freshman Class, which is composed of thirty (30) members, and three other small classes. But the size of the Freshman class is a most satisfactory guarantee of the number which will fill the halls of the University so soon as the students are qualified and set in order in the several classes. When the four classes are all full by regular promotion we shall have in these courses at least one hundred and twenty (120) students. This will be but the result of natural growth, as the classes from the Preparatory School are elevated to the places occupied by the students now in the University. To reach this result will require three years. Before that time has passed the number of our students in the upper classes cannot be materially increased.

The result of this state of things in the past year would have been an imperfect division of labor among the Professors, but that those Professors whose work lies chiefly in the upper classes, which are small, have, with great alacrity, assisted in the instruction of the lower classes, or in the Preparatory School.

This has been the case specially with the Professors in the Departments of Natural, Moral and Mental Sciences, and of the Modern Languages.

These Professors have assisted with marked success in the instruction given to the Preparatory School, and to the Sub-Freshman Class, and in the Ancient Languages, as indicated by their reports, while the Professors in the Mathematics, the Ancient Languages, History, and specially the English Department, have done full work, as will be seen in their reports.

With regard to the granting of State aid to students who are below the standard for entrance into the University, as set forth by the four years' college courses, the majority of the Faculty have acted upon the principle that it is better, if the State is to help the student at all, she should assist at the beginning of his course. She must aid him into College, and through his first two or three years, or not aid him at all. Then, the student having received this assistance, and having obtained a more advanced education, will be able to go out, and by serving the State in the capacity of a teacher or by similar work may obtain the means to complete his course. We have heard the Superintendent of Education lately, mention in public the fact that our scholarship students in the upper classes have done most satisfactory work in this respect by teaching school during the last summer. It must be plain that if such students cannot obtain some assistance which will enable them to live in the place where they may enjoy the benefits of the State University and State Normal School, they can hope for little aid to that end from those all-absorbing employments in which an ignorant man must engage in order to obtain a livelihood.

On the other hand, the State cannot afford to throw away money on teachers who have not acquired an education sufficient to fit them for the University or the Normal School; but she can afford the necessary aid to fit them for those institutions, and then send them out to be teachers or to engage in such appropriate employments as may enable them to return and complete their studies. It must be remembered, also, that until the County High Schools are established and get into full working order, all students who are remanded by the Board of State Examiners to their homes are left to remain in places and positions where they can obtain no instruction which will fit them for either our College Department or for the Normal School.

If we could place them in our Preparatory School and keep them there, that would, without doubt, be the best course; but they cannot stay here and attend the Preparatory School. It will be noticed that there are only two in the Sub-Freshman Class on scholarship from the city of Columbia. The rest are from the outlying Counties.

In conclusion, I trust this report will be accepted, with its accompanying documents, as a satisfactory account of the condition and work of the University, as well as a defense of its position in the educational system of the State and country.

Respectfully submitted.

BENJAMIN B. BABBITT,
Chairman of the Faculty.

APPENDIX I.—*List of Students in the University who have been admitted to Scholarships, together with their Ages, Studies and Marks.*

	NAME OF STUDENT.	RESIDENCE.	AGE.	CLASS.	STUDIES EXAMINED IN.	GENERAL AVERAGE.
1	Cardozo, I. N.	Charleston	18	Freshman / Classical	Latin, Greek, Algebra, Geometry, History, Rhetoric	90
2	Dart, W. M.	Charleston	21	Junior / Classical	French, German, Natural Philosophy, Mental and Moral Philosophy, Mathematics, English Literature, Chemistry	86
3	Townsend, A. G.	Charleston	21	Junior / Classical	French, German, Natural Philosophy, Mental and Moral Philosophy, Mathematics, English Literature, Chemistry	85
4	Morris, J. M.	Charleston	22	Junior / Classical	French, German, Natural Philosophy, Mental and Moral Philosophy, Mathematics, English Literature, Chemistry	83
5	Shippen, P. W.	Columbia	19	Freshman / Classical	Latin, Greek, Algebra, Geometry, History and Rhetoric	81
6	Lay, J. F.	Anderson	20	Freshman / Classical	French, German, Algebra, Geometry, History and Rhetoric	80
7	Saltus, Thad.	Columbia	24	Freshman / Classical	Latin, Greek, Algebra, Geometry, History and Rhetoric	79
8	Hazel, P. V.	Charleston	18	Freshman / Classical	Latin, Greek, Algebra, Geometry, History and Rhetoric	78
9	McKinney, C.	Columbia	19	Freshman / Classical	Latin, Greek, Algebra, Geometry, History and Rhetoric	78
10	Shrewsbury, W. H.	Charleston	18	Freshman / Classical	Latin, Greek, Algebra, Geometry, History and Rhetoric	75
11	Scott, C. C.	Charleston	20	Sophomore / Classical	Latin, Greek, Nat.Philosophy, Mathematics, History, Rhetoric	74
12	Puckett, I. D.	Walhalla	18	Sophomore / Classical	French, German, Algebra, Geometry, History and Rhetoric	74
13	Purcell, I. I.	Winnsboro	17	Freshman	Latin, Greek, Algebra, Geometry, History and Rhetoric	73
14	McLain, T. A.	Charleston	21	Sophomore / Classical	Latin, Greek, Nat.Philosophy, Mathematics, History, Rhetoric	72
15	McKinlay, W.	Charleston	17	Freshman	Latin, Greek, Algebra, Geometry, History and Rhetoric	72

List of Students in the University who have been Admitted to Scholarships, &c.—Continued.

	Name of Student.	Residence.	Age.	Class.	Studies Examined In.	General Average.
16	McLaurin, M.	Marlboro	22	Freshman.	Latin, French, Algebra, Geometry, History and Rhetoric	72
17	Middleton, N. H.	Barnwell	19	Freshman.	French, German, Algebra, Geometry, History and Rhetoric	72
18	Roberts, T. F. P.	Charleston	16	Freshman.	Latin, Greek, Algebra, Geometry, History and Rhetoric	71
19	Scott, L. D.	Columbia	21	Freshman.	Latin, Greek, Algebra, Geometry, History and Rhetoric	70
20	Seay, J. H.	Lexington	23	Freshman.	French, German, Algebra, Geometry, History and Rhetoric	70
21	O'Hear, J. M.	Charleston	19	Freshman, Classical	Latin, Greek, Algebra, Geometry, History and Rhetoric	70
22	Stewart, E. J.	Newberry	20	Freshman.	Latin, Greek, Algebra, Geometry, History and Rhetoric	68
23	Varne, J. G.	Barnwell	19	Freshman.	French, German, Algebra, Geometry, History and Rhetoric	75
24	Stewart, T. McC.	Charleston	22	Senior	German, Mental and Moral Philosophy, Natural Philosophy, Geology, English Literature, Ev. of Christianity, Pol. Economy.	68
25	Davis, N. C.	York	19	Freshman.	Latin, French, Algebra, Geometry, History, Rhetoric	67
26	Dixon, G. W.	Orangeburg	19	Freshman.	French, German, Algebra, Geometry, History, Rhetoric	66
27	Dart, J. L.	Charleston	21	Freshman, Classical	Latin, Greek, Algebra, Geometry, History, Rhetoric	65
28	Williams, G. D.	Anderson	25	Freshman.	Latin, French, Algebra, Geometry, History, Rhetoric	65
29	Evans, T. R.	Chesterfield	17	Freshman.	Latin, French, Algebra, Geometry, History, Rhetoric	61
30	Smith, O. L. W.	Aiken	23	Freshman.	Latin, French, Algebra, Geometry, History, Rhetoric	60
31	Stewart, C. D.	Charleston	17	Freshman.	Latin, Greek, Algebra, Geometry, History, Rhetoric	59
32	Parmelee, C. R.	Columbia	15	Freshman, Classical	Latin, Greek, Algebra, Geometry, Rhetoric, History	55
33	Posey, L. O.	Aiken	23	Freshman.	French, German, Algebra, Geometry, Rh:toric, History	52
34	Williams, W. J.	Edgefield	19	Freshman.	French, German, Algebra, Geometry, Rhetoric, History	50

List of Students in the University who have been admitted to Scholarships, &c.—Concluded.

SUB-FRESHMAN CLASS.

	NAME OF STUDENT.	RESIDENCE.	AGE	CLASS.	STUDIES EXAMINED IN.	GENERAL AVERAGE.
35	Henderson, F. H.	Newberry	15	Sub-Freshman.	Latin, Greek, Arithmetic, Algebra, History	87
36	McCoy, S. H.	Columbia	17	"	"	87
37	Kershaw, H. B.	Darlington	17	"	"	83
38	Whittaker, J. C.	Kershaw	16	"	"	83
39	Johnston, J. H.	Kershaw	19	"	"	78
40	Murray, G. W.	Anderson	20	"	"	78
41	Simkins, J. A.	Edgefield	19	"	"	75
42	Oliver, J. L.	Columbia	16	"	"	73
43	Williams, J. L.	Orangeburg	16	"	"	73
44	Sinclair, W. A.	Georgetown	18	"	"	72
45	McMorris, Z. W.	Newberry	22	"	"	71
46	Hart, G. E.	Orangeburg	19	"	"	70
47	Clinton, G. W. C.	Lancaster	15	"	"	69
48	Holland, J. J.	Georgetown	15	"	"	69
49	Goosely, A.	Columbia	25	"	"	63
50	Durham, J. J.	Greenville	22	"	"	62
51	Smith, A. S.	Darlington	23	"	"	62
52	Durant, A. H.	Marion	23	"	"	59
53	Young, K. M.	Spartanburg	17	"	"	57
54	Lee, R. O.	Winnsboro	20	"	"	53
55	Simmons, Benj.	Beaufort	22	"	"	53
56	Lawrence, M. B.	Admitted to a scholarship, but at home on leave, without the benefit of the scholarship.				
57	Pinckney, —	"		"		

APPENDIX II.

Questions for Examination for Scholarships, October, 1874.

ENGLISH GRAMMAR.

1. What is English Grammar?
2. Define a sentence, and give an example. What must every sentence contain?
3. Name the parts of speech. How many numbers, genders, cases and persons are there?
4. Give the feminine of *hero*. Compare *full*.
5. Give the principal parts of the verb *to see*.
6. Parse the following sentence: "The accusing angel flew up to Heaven's chancery with the oath, and blushed as he gave it in."

ARITHMETIC.

1. What letters are used in the Roman method of Notation? and what is the value of each in numbers?
2. Express in words the value of DCXCIX.
3. How do you prove Division?
4. What is an abstract number?
5. What are integers?
6. What kind of a fraction is $\frac{2}{3}$ of $\frac{1}{4}$ of $2\frac{2}{3}$ of $\frac{1}{7}$, and what is its value reduced to a simple fraction?
7. What is the sum of $\frac{2}{5}$, $\frac{1}{3}$, $\frac{1}{4}$ and $\frac{9}{10}$?
8. Reduce $\dfrac{\frac{5}{9}}{3}$ to a simple fraction.
9. From 125.26 take 57.508.
10. Reduce .025 to a common fraction.
11. From 6 T. 14 cwt. 2 qr. 20 lbs. 12 oz., take 4 T. 17 cwt. 1 qr. 21 lbs. 10 oz.
12. What is the interest on $850 for 1 year 7 mo. 18 days at 7 per cent. per annum?
13. What is reduction?
14. What is proportion?
15. State and solve by proportion the following:
    If 9 hats cost $45, how many hats can you buy for $175?

16. Analyze the following questions, viz : If $\frac{5}{9}$ of a man's age is 35 years, how old is he ?

17. Reduce $27\frac{3}{4}$ to a fraction.

18. A man by selling his plantation for $800 lost 20 per cent., what was the plantation worth ?

19. Extract the square root of 7569.

20. Extract the cube root of 2744.

GREEK GRAMMAR.

1. Decline *polites logos* the article *'o.*
2. Inflect *Luo* first aorist, active, indicative.
3. Give the future of *prasso gignosko 'istemi.*

The remainder of the examination in Latin and Greek will be oral.

LATIN GRAMMAR.

1. Decline *ager, animal, mitis.*
2. Compare *bonus, fucilis.*
3. Give the principal parts of *cresco, do, rogo.*
4. Give the three roots of *audio, amo.*

CÆSAR.

1. Translate—

Cæsar his de causis, quas commemoravi, Rhenum transire decreverat; sed navibus tranpire neque satis tutum esse arbitrabatur, neque suæ neque populi Romani dignitatis esse statuebat; itaque, etsi summa difficultas faciundi pontis proponebatur propter latitudinem, rapiditatem, altitudinemque fluminis, tamen id sibi contendendum, aut aliter non transducendum exercitum, existimabat.

2. Parse *his, quas, naribus, dignitatis, pontis, sibi, exercitum.*

·ALGEBRA.

1. What is Algebra?

2. When the quantities are similar in Algebra, but the signs unlike, how do you add ?

3. From $3a^2$ take $(3a-x+y.)$

4. Divide $a^3-3a^2y+3ay^2-y^3$ by $a-y.$

5. Reduce $5x\dfrac{2x+5}{x+2}$ to a fraction.

6. Given $\dfrac{x}{2}-3+\dfrac{x}{3}=5-3$ to find value of $x.$

7. Given $x : x-a :: a : c$, to find value of $x.$

2

8. One-half of a post is in the earth, one-third in the water, and the remainder, which is 3 feet, above the water, how high is the post?

9. What is the cube of $2a-3y$?

10. Given $\left\{ \begin{array}{l} 2x+\ 3y=\ 7 \\ 8x+10y=26 \end{array} \right\}$ to find the value of x and y.

GEOGRAPHY.

1. How many zones are there, and where are they situated?

2. Bound the United States, and give the Capital.

3. What are the principal mountain ranges of the United States? Which of them are east, and which west, of the Mississippi River?

4. Give the names of the principal rivers of the United States.

5. By what route can we travel by water from Cincinnati to Charleston?

6. What are the names of the largest lakes of North America?

7. Name the three principal islands of the West Indies.

8. Where are the following cities: Pekin, Cairo, Rio Janeiro, Vienna?

9. Name the five principal countries of Europe.

10. Where is Madagascar?

AMERICAN HISTORY.

1. When was the Declaration of Independence adopted?

2. To what nation did the principal colonies of North America belong at the time of the Revolution?

3. What event closed the war of the Revolution?

4. Who was President of the United States during the war of 1812?

5. When did the war of the Rebellion begin, and when did it end?

APPENDIX III.

Reports of the Several Professors and Officers of the University.

THE SCHOOL OF NATURAL PHILOSOPHY, &c.

In making my report on the Department committed specially to my care, I have to say that its condition is far from what it should be, and that I have been greatly hindered in the proper work of instruction by the duties of my office as Chairman of the Faculty, and the condition of the apparatus. It is antiquated in its style, unfit for use from age and infirmity, and demands constant repairs.

The labor which is required in the workshop to get ready for recitation and lectures, is double what it should be, and I have no proper assistant.

Having no solid table on which to set the apparatus while displaying it during the recitation and lecture, I have myself set up a counter which is not subject to the jar of the floor, and have also built a closet, in which the noxious fumes of the galvanic battery pass off up the chimney.

Larger appropriations are needed for more modern apparatus, and for the construction of more convenient arrangements in the recitation room.

I have not yet been able, in those classes which I have instructed during the past year, to carry them at all into the Mathematics of Natural Philosopy. The Junior Class has recited with the Sophomore Class and the Senior has undertaken what belongs to both the Senior and Junior year.

The Sophomore have thus far gone over the construction of bodies, and the effects of heat on their volume and condition, and the mechanism of solids; the several subjects being considered specially with regard to their phenomena and their laws.

The Senior class has been instructed in Natural Philosophy, the Metaphysics of Natural Philosophy and the Theory of Mechanics, and is just now entering upon the mathematical application of mechanical principles. These, in their application to the celestial movements, will constitute the course for the rest of the year.

In Natural Philosophy, I have used as a text book the latest edition of Olmstead.

The five students in the Sophomore Class have four recitations and lectures per week.

The four students in the Junior have three.

The two Seniors have three recitations per week.

I have also had the Senior Class three times in the week in Evidences of Christianity.

I use in this class Butler's Analogy for a text book, having gone over the first part of the evidences of Natural Religion, with lectures on the subject of "The Existence of a Personal God."

The Sub-Freshman Class have also recited to me three times in the week in the Arithmetic. They are 23 in number.

With them I use Sanford's Arithmetic, and have carried them through Partial Payments, expecting to complete the arithmetic before the end of the year.

The examination papers for the February examination are herewith presented.

BENJ. B. BABBITT,
Professor of Natural Philosopy, &c.

NATURAL PHILOSOPHY.

SOPHOMORE AMD JUNIOR QUESTIONS.

1. What is the particular province of Natural Philosphy? and what are its chief divisions?

2. Define Extension, Impenetrability, Divisibility Compressibility, Elasticity, Attraction.

3. How are bodies measured which are regular in their form? Describe the several standards of measurement?

4. How are irregular bodies measured?

5. Describe some of the methods for obtaining specific gravity and give the principle.

6. What are the effects of heat upon bodies in respect to magnitude and condition.

7. Define Latent and Specific Heat.

8. Define the co-efficients of expansion, linear, superficial, cubical, apparent and real.

9. Describe the different gradings of thermometers, and the principle involved in their construction and use.

10. What is the maximun tension of vapors and the dew point?

11. Describe the action and give the principle of the steam engine.

12. What are the several phenomena of adhesion and cohesion?

13. Define motion, momentum and *vis viva* or moving energy.

14. State the three laws of motion and by whom discovered.

15. Define composition and resolution of forces.

16. Define gravity. State the laws of falling bodies.

17. Describe the pendulum. State the principles involved in its action. Describe its uses.

18. State the principle of the lever, the law of equal moments. Describe the pulley, and state the principle on which it rests.

19. Describe the inclined plane, and state its principle.

20. What are the forces involved in the movements of rotation and revolution, and what are some of the phenomena which attends these motions.

NATURAL PHILOSOPHY.

SENIORS.

1. What kind of reasoning is used in Natural Philosophy?

2. Define observation, experiment, phenomena, hypothesis and theory.

3. What is constitution of material bodies, and how are they put together?

4. In what three senses is the term crystaline form used, and how are crystals generated?

5. Describe the action of Friction.

6. Describe the action of storms of various kinds. Their movements and the methods of their production.

7. Describe the various phenomena which arise from the presence of moisture in the atmosphere.

8. Describe the behavior of the important currents in the ocean, and of the effect of these currents on climate.

9. How was the mechanical equivalent of heat estimated, and by whom?

10. What evidence is there of the existence of the Ether?

11. Define force, pressure, power and energy.

12. Give the three laws of motion.

13. Give the equations for accelerating motion from rest, from an original motion and for retarded motion.

14. Describe some of the actual effects of Cohesion.

15. The rule for calculating the problems of Re-action and Action.

EVIDENCES OF CHRISTIANITY.

BUTLER'S ANALOGY.

1. Illustrate the fact that Butler's Analogy is an argument from Induction, and show how he proves—

First. A future life.

Second. The state of probation, as implying trial, difficulties and danger as intended for moral discipline and improvement.

2. What is his argument respecting the opinion of necessity as influencing practice?

3. What is his argument in regard to our imperfect comprehension of the government of God as affecting our duty?

4. Define personal existence.

In what manner would you answer the following sentences in Mr. Tyndall's Address, delivered at Belfast last August?

5. First. "The theories of the ancients took an anthropomorphic form."

6. Second. "Tested by observation and reflection these early notions failed in the long run to satisfy the most penetrating intellects of our race."

7. Third. "As science demands the radical extirpation of caprice, and the absolute reliance upon law in nature, there grew with the growth of scientific notions a desire and determination to sweep from the field of theory this mob of gods and demons, and to place natural phenomena on a basis more congruent with themselves."

8. Fourth. "If you will apprehend and keep in mind the grand conception of the atoms, nature, free, at once, and rid of her haughty lords, is seen to do all things spontaneously of herself without the meddling of the gods."

9. Fifth. "Matter is not the mere naked, empty capacity which philosophers have pictured her to be, but the universal mother, who brings forth all things as the fruit of her own womb."

10. Sixth. "It is the mind thus stored, as was Darwin's mind, with the choicest materials of the Teleologist, that rejects Teleology, seeking to refer these wonders to natural causes. They, according to him, illustrate the method of nature, and not the technic of a manlike artificer."

11. Seventh. "The definitions of matter given in our text books were intended to cover its purely physical and mechanical properties, * * but are the definitions complete? * * I discern in matter which we, in our ignorance, notwithstanding our professed reverence for its Creator, have hitherto covered with opprobrium, the promise and potency of every form and quality of life."

12. Eighth. "When the conception that all we see around us, and all we feel within us, the phenomena of physical nature, as well as those of the human mind, have their unsearchable roots in a cosmical existence * * of which only an infinitessimal span is offered to the investigation of man, and this span is only knowable in part, &c."

SUB-FRESHMAN ARITHMETIC.

1. Define Addition, Subtraction, Multiplication and Division.

2. What is the greatest common divisor and the least common multipler of 4, 8, 16?

3. In what ways may Division be expressed?

4. Add $\frac{2}{3}$ of $\frac{5}{6}$ $3\frac{7}{8}$, $4\frac{7}{16}$, $3\frac{2}{3}$ and $\frac{\frac{7}{8}}{\frac{3}{4}}$

5. Multiply $17569\frac{5}{6}$ by $328\frac{4}{5}$

6. Divide $47689\frac{1}{4}$ by $33\frac{7}{10}$

7. Add ten billion one hundred and ten, and the decimal one-ten thousandth.

Seven hundred and fifty-six thousand and one hundred and seventy-five, and the decimal four hundred and fifty-seven hundred-thousandths.

One hundred and forty-five millions five hundred and sixty-seven thousand and the decimal thirty-seven thousandths.

Write the sum total in words.

8. Multiply 367.25 by 2. 7.

9. Divide 25 by 5, also 2.5 by 5, also 25 by .005.

10. How much kerosine oil in 9 'barrels each containing 42 gallons, 3 quarts, 1 pint, 3 gills?

11. A gardener put 5 bushels 3 pecks 7 quarts of tomatoes into 21 boxes, how much did each box hold?

12. A man sold a carriage for $280.56 and thereby lost 16 per cent. of the cost. What did the carriage cost?

13. [$336.84.]   Nashville, Tenn., April 5, 1871.

On demand, with interest from date at 6 per cent., I promise to pay John Daily or order, for value received, the sum of three hundred and thirty-six and $84\frac{84}{100}$ dollars.

What was the value of this note July 15, 1872?

14. Note dated   Richmond, Va., February 8, 1868.

Face of the note $720, rate 6 per cent.

Credits endorsed Dec. 23, 1868, $207.

Oct. 3, 1868,   20.

Aug. 13, 1870,   18.

Dec. 23, 1870, 300.

What was the balance due April 28, 1871?

SCHOOL OF MATHEMATICS.

University of South Carolina.

A. W. Cummings, A. M., D. D. Pfofessor.

To Reverend B. B. Babbitt, *A. M., Chairman of the Faculty:*

Sir :—I have the honor to report, that the matriculates in this school are divided into three classes, Freshman, Sophomores, Juniors. The freshman class embraces twenty-nine regular and one special student.

This is the largest class that has entered the institution since the year 1859.

This class has in this school six recitations a week, as follows: On Mondays, Wednesdays and Fridays, Geometry, and on Tuesdays, Thursdays and Saturdays, Algebra.

The monthly grade ranged from 57 to 94, and the monthly average for the whole class was 74, the maximum being 100.

The range of values obtained at the intermediate examination was from 56 to 97, the average of the whole class was 75.

Only two students fell below 60 and 19 of them stood above 70. It is thus seen that every member of this class ranks above medium, and three of them attain to first honor.

The class will complete Robinson's University Algebra and Geometry before the end of the term in June, 1875.

In the Sophomore class there are five students, four of them taking the full classical course, and one the modern course, which substitutes French and German for Latin and Greek.

This class has completed Robinson's University plane trigonometry, and passed a good examination on it, they have gone over right angled spherical trigonometry, they will complete during the year trigonometry, plane and spherical, mensuration, and land surveying, theoretical and practical. This class grade from 68 to 85, averaging 77.

There have been five students in the Junior Mathematical class, one of whom has recently transferred to the law school. The class has completed and been examined on spherical trigonometry, and gone over about one-third of Conic Sections. They will complete Conic Sections and Analytical Geometry during the term. They attained from 72 to 88, at the late examination, making an average of 85 per cent.

The text books in use in this school are Robinson's University editions. They are very full and well up to the present standards of mathematical science. No instance of disorder, requiring even the mildest rebuke, has occurred in my department; a desire to improve has characterized every student.

Taking into account former opportunities, and the great number of studies in other schools, the progress of the poorest in my classes has been all that I could have expected. The examination papers of this school at the late examination are hereunto appended.

I have the honor to be your obedient servant,

A. W. CUMMINGS.

MATHEMATICS.

SEMI-ANNUAL EXAMINATION, FEBRUARY, 1875.

FRESHMAN CLASS.

Prof. A. W. Cummings.

ALGEBRA.

1. What is an equation ? What are the transformations of an equation, and how is an equation cleared of denominators ?—(4.)

2. How many methods of elimination are there, and what are they ?—(4.)

3. What is the sign of infinity, and what is the expression for an infinite quantity divided by a finite ?—(4.)

4. What is the expression $\frac{0}{b}$ equal to ?—(4.)

5. If 2 or more inequalities subsisting in the same sense be added, member to member, what will be the result ?—(4.)

6. What will be the effect upon the sign, and what the result if an inequality be subtracted from an equation ?—(4.)

7. Give the rule for writing out the square of a polynomial, without the form of actual involution.—(4.)

8. Find the value of x in the equation

$$\frac{3x}{4} - \frac{x-1}{2} = 6x - \frac{20x + 13}{141}.—(4.)$$

9. An estate was divided among 4 children, in such a way that the *first* received $200 more than ⅓ of the whole ; the *second* $340 more than ⅕ of the whole ; the *third* $300 more than ⅙ of the whole, and the *fourth* $400 more than ⅔ of the whole, what was the value of the estate ?—(5.)

10. A can perform a piece of work in 8 days, B, in 12 days, in how many days can they perform it, both working together ?—(7.)

11. Given $\begin{aligned} 3x+7y&=70 \text{ and} \\ x+4y&=38 \end{aligned}$ to find x and y.—(7.)

12. Find the value of each letter in the following :

$$U+v+x+y+2z=52$$
$$U+v+x+z+2y=50$$
$$U+v+y+z+2x=48$$
$$U+x+y+z+2v=46$$
$$V+x+y+z+2u=44.—(7.)$$

13. Find x in the example $\dfrac{3x}{4} - \dfrac{x-1}{2} < 6x - \dfrac{20x+13}{4}$ (7.)

14. By the short process, square the polynomial $a+b+c+d+f=$ what?

15. Find the value of $(a^4 - a^3b + 3a^2b^2 - ab^3 + b^4)^{\frac{1}{2}} =$ what ?—(9.)
$$\overline{\quad\quad\quad\quad 4 \quad\quad 4 \quad\quad 1b\quad}$$

16. Find the value of $\sqrt[3]{27a^3 + 108a^2 + 244a + 64} =$ what ?—(10.)

17. $\sqrt{\dfrac{(\sqrt{5}+2)\ (\sqrt[4]{5}+\sqrt{2})\ (\sqrt[4]{5}+\sqrt{2})}{(\sqrt{13}+2)\ (\sqrt[4]{13}+\sqrt{3})\ (\sqrt[4]{13}+\sqrt{3})}} =$ what ? (10.)

Total 100.

SOPHOMORE CLASS—PLANE TRIGONOMETRY.

1. What is trigonometry, and what plane trigonometry ?—(8).

2. What is a degree ?—(8).

3. What is the complement, supplement, sine, cosine, tangent, cotangent, secant and cosecant of an arc ?—(8).

4. Demonstrate that $R^2 = Sin^2 + cosine^2$ —(8).

5. Prove that tang. $= \dfrac{\text{sin,}}{\text{cos}}$ and that tang $= \dfrac{1}{\text{cotangt.}} \Big\}$ —(10).

6. Demonstrate that the sines of angles are to each other as the sides opposite them.—(10.)

7. Demonstrate that the chord of 60°, and tang. of 45° are each equal to Radius, and that the sine of 30°, the versed sine of 60°, and cosin of 60° are each equal to one-half of Radius.—(12).

8. In any right angled triangle, let the hypotenuse equal 331 rods, the angle at the base equal 49° 14′ to find the other parts.—(12.)

9. In an oblique triangle, let the angles at the base be 70° 51′ 22″ and 59° 35′ 36″, a side opposite the last angle = 720, 8 rods, to find the other parts.—(12.)

10. Let each side of a triangle = 100,3 to find the three angles.—(12.)

JUNIOR CLASS—SPHERICAL TRIGONOMETRY.

1. What is the object of spherical trigonometry ?

2. How many circular parts, and what is the middle part ?

3. What are Napier's rules for the solution of spherical triangles ?

4. How are right angled triangles, oblique angled triangles and quadrantal triangles solved ?

5. In the right angled sph. triangle A B C, given A B 47° 26′ 35″ the A C. 118° 32′ 12″ to find the other parts.

6. In a quadrantal triangle, given the quadrantal side 90° one angle adjacent 118° 40′ 36″, and a side opposite the last angle mentioned 113° 2′ 28″ to find the other parts.

7. In an oblique angled spher., triangle, given the side a 77° 25′ 11″, side C 128° 14′ 47″ and the angle C 131° 11′ 12″ to find the other parts, Nos. 1, 2, 3 and 4, above, each valued 10=40; 5, 6 and 7 each, valued 20=60=100.

REPORT OF DEPARTMENT OF HISTORY.

COLUMBIA, S. C., February 22, 1875.

Prof. B. B. BABBITT, *Chairman of the Faculty of the University of South Carolina:*

SIR—I herewith submit the following report in regard to the Department of History:

I have under my charge three classes, namely, the Sub-Freshman, Freshman and Senior classes, the first of which numbers twenty-three (23) scholars, and the second thirty (30.)

These three classes I have had under my charge for the first term of the present scholastic year, and I have to report that they have been diligent in their studies, and have made a constant and steady progress in acquiring a competent knowledge of history.

The text-books used are Freeman's Outlines of Universal History for Sub-Freshman class, and Talheimer's Manual of History for the Freshman class.

Both of these classes have made considerable progress in the books mentioned.

I would also state that these two large classes, exhibiting the average grade of mind in this Institution, have shown a good standard of scholarship during the Intermediate Examination.

In regard to the Senior Class who have been pursuing the study of Political Economy during the first term of this scholastic year, I have to state that they have nearly completed this subject of study, and have attained a high grade of scholarship upon the late Intermediate Examination.

The text-book used in this branch of study is Thorold Rogers' Manual of Political Economy, in connection with a course of reading in larger works upon the subject, such as Fawcett and Mill.

The full studies of this Department, when all the classes are engaged, will be in order, as follows: Outlines of Universal History, Political Philosophy, Political Economy, Social Science, etc.

Yours very respectfully,

T. N. ROBERTS.

P. S.—Find appended to this report copies of questions in Political Economy and History to the Freshman, Sub-Freshman and Senior Classes.

INTERMEDIATE EXAMINATION IN POLITICAL ECONOMY, FEBRUARY, 1875.

SENIORS.

1. What are the three elements of wealth; and what is understood by the cost of production?—(Value 5.)

2. Describe the effects of co-operation and division of labor, and in general terms the effect of the introduction of machinery upon labor; also, whether a general rise or fall of prices is possible?—(Value 8.)

3. What is meant by a measure of value? also, describe the origin and function of money; and, further, describe some of the substitutes for gold and silver; finally state some of the effects which would result from a double currency.—(Value 8.)

4. What is capital, wages and profit? Can credit take the place of capital?—(Value 5.)

5. Describe the theory of Malthus in regard to population.—(Value 5.)

6. Describe the theories of free trade and production.—(Value 10.)

7. Describe the mode of operation of Trades' Unions, and state what economical results follow their action. Further, show what results may follow a system of co-operation.—(Value 10.)

8. Describe some of the Tenancies of Land in different countries; also, Ricardo's Theory of Rent.—(Value 5.)

9. Give the rules of Adam Smith in regard to taxation; and, also, describe the respective advantages of direct and indirect taxation.—(Value 8.)

10. What arguments may be advanced to show that Political Economy is a science, and that the reasoning of M. Comte is false in regard to this study being inexact and arbitrary in its conclusions. Further, describe why there has been an assumed connection between the theory of Laisez-faire, and the development of Political Economy?—(Value 14.)

11. Shifting our argument to another stand-point, can there be a science of Politocal Economy founded on principles of abstract justice and right. Give the argument.—(Value 12.)

12. Describe some of the phases of Modern Socialism; especially as shown in the character of the International. Further, has Political Economy followed the laws of universal progress.—(Value 10.)

SUB-FRESHMAN CLASS.

HISTORY.

1. Describe the great race-groups of mankind, known as the Historic races. Also, state what races of men make up the sub-group called Aryan; and, further, describe the order of their migration from Asia into Europe.—(Value 8.)

2. Describe the origin of the Greco-Latin Race; also, the character of the early Greeks; the spirit of the Constitutions of Athens and Sparta. Also, describe the manner of electing the ancient Kings in Greece; the power of the Aristocracy, and the growth of the Democratic power. Describe the results of the Persian invasion; also, the Peloponnesian war and its results.—(Value 10.)

3. Describe the origin of the city of Rome, and the extension of its power over Latium, and, finally, over Italy. Describe the wars of Rome with Carthage, Macedonia, Mithridates, and the civil war between Pompeius and Cæsar. Also, describe the final consolidation and supremacy of Roman power over the world.—(Value 12.)

4. Describe the character of Cæsar, and the extent and power of the Empire under Augustus. Also, give an account of the reign of Constantine, and of his conversion to Christianty. Further, describe the decline of the Roman power, the several Teutonic invasions, and its final overthrow by the Northern barbarians. Finally, give an account of the influence of Roman civilization upon the nations of Europe.—(Value 15.)

5. Describe the Eastern Roman Empire, and its influence in History. (Value 5.)

6. Describe the rise and fall of the Saracenic power. Also, describe the Frankish Empire of Charlamagne, and name some of the nations which followed upon the dissolution of his power. Describe, specifically, the origin of the Kingdom of England and France.—(Value 12.)

7. Give an account of the growth of the Papal power, the diffusion of Christianity over Europe, and the growth of the Monastic orders.— (Value 10.)

8. Give an account of the Normans, and of their settlement in Normandy; and, also, of the Norman conquest of England. Also, describe the growth of the Romance nations and languages.—(Value 8.)

9. Give an account of the origin and growth of the Feudal system, and of Chivalry; and the effects of the Crusades.—(Value 10.)

10. Give a general description of the middle ages.— (Value 10.)

FRESHMAN CLASS.

HISTORY.

1. Describe the chief groups into which mankind is subdivided. Also, describe the migration of the Ayran nations into Europe, in the order of time, and the different countries they occupied.—(Value 12.)

2. Give a general account of the history of Egypt, its antiquity, traditions and early growth. Describe the Egyptian religion, science and art; also, state how the people were divided for industrial and other purposes. Also, offer an estimate of the influence of this ancient civilization upon the history of the nations of antiquity.—(Value 15.)

3. Describe the ancient Chaldeans, and give the leading characteristics of their civilization, and a description of their early progress in science.— (Value 5.)

4. Describe the Assyrian Monarchy; the extent of its power over other nations, and some of the peculiar characteristics of its people, and the memorials left of its former power.—(Value 8.)

5. Describe the rise and fall of the Median Monarchy; the power of the Magi, and the splendor of the Court of Ecbatana.—(Value 5.)

6. Describe the origin of the Babylonian Empire; the extent of its dominion at the height of its power; the character of its civilization, and the genius of its people in government, science, art and commerce.— (Value 10.)

7. Describe the history of the kingdoms of Israel and Judah, and the mission of the Jewish people in history.—(Value 5.)

8. Describe the rise, growth, and final extent of power of the Persian Empire. Also, describe in what manner the Persians made the nearest approach, of any Asiatic people, towards those traits of civilization called European. Further, describe the Persian religion, and how it finally became corrupt. Finally, state how the power of Persia was overthrown, and became merged in that of another nation.—(Value 15.)

9. Describe the early history of Greece, the form of the more primitive governments, and the character of the ancient Grecian races. Also, name what Hellenic State first attained a high political development in philosophy, science, art and government; the character of its civilization, and the influence it exerted upon all the other Grecian States. Describe the Peloponnesian war; its character and results. Further, describe the character of the State which acquired power in the Peloponnesus, and the nature of the influence it exerted over the rest of Greece. Finally, give an estimate of the influence of Grecian civilization over the ancient world, and show how its effects, directly and afterwards, through Roman civilization, have been continued to this time.—(Value 20.)

10. Describe the rise of Macedonian power over Greece.—(Value 5.)

———

UNIVERSITY CAMPUS, February 20, 1875.
To Rev. B. B. BABBITT, A. M., Chairman of the Faculty:

DEAR SIR—In the department of Rhetoric and English Literature, of which I have the honor to have charge, instruction has been given during the term ending February 15, 1875, as follows:

1. *Senior Class.*—This class, consisting of two members, and one added from the department of Law, has had weekly recitations in Taine's English Literature, review of themes, and weekly lectures on the English Poets,

in all 18 recitations. The result of the intermediate examination shows marked proficency, the average being 81.

2. *Junior Class,* consisting of three members. There have been semi-weekly recitations in Taine's English Literature, and review of themes. Forty recitations. At the intermediate examination this class made an average of 91½.

3. *Sophomore Class.*—Five members. Weekly recitations in Whately's Rhetoric, and weekly lectures on English Composition. Forty recitations. Average 83.

4. *Freshman Class.*—Two divisions. First division, 17 members. Second division, 13 members. Each division one weekly recitation in Rhetoric, and weekly lecture on Prose Composition. Sixty recitations during the term, with average of 72 at intermediate examination.

5. *Sub-Freshman Class.*—Two divisions. First division, 12 members. Second division, 12 members. Weekly recitations in Syntax, and weekly lecture on English Language. In all 74 recitations. Average marks at intermediate examination 67.

In addition to the above, which embrace all the regular duties of the professor in this Department, I have given a weekly lecture to the 78 boys of the Preparatory School on Physical Geography; heard the semi-weekly recitations of a class in Ancient History, and also delivered a semi-weekly lecture on Elocution to the 28 students attending the Normal School.

Summary for the term ending February 15, 1875: I have given instruction in my Department to no less than 171 persons, attended 222 recitations and delivered 170 lectures—each lecture requiring a full hour for its delivery. The discipline of the various classes has been all that I could desire or expect. I have every reason to believe that this large, not to say excessive, amount of labor has been fruitful of good results. I append examination papers, and remain,

Respectfully, your colleague,

HENRY J. FOX,

Professor of Rhetoric, Criticism, Elocution, and

English Language and Literature.

JUNIORS AND SENIORS.

TAINE'S ENGLISH LITERATURE.

1. Where did the Saxons originate; what were their mental characteristics and physical peculiarities?

2. Who were the Normans, and how did they affect literature?

3. For what was Chaucer distinguished?

4. Render the following into modern English, and name its author:

3

The dore was all of athamant eterne, yclenched overthwart and endelong with yren tough, and for to make it strong, every piler the temple to sustene was tonne-gret of yens bright and shene.

5. Give a passage illustrative of the power of Shakespeare's imagination.

6. A passage illustrative of the barbarity of the times.

7. How does the author characterise Milton's "Jehovah?"

8. Milton's "Adam and Eve?"

9. Milton's "Satan?"

10. What was Milton's "Hell" as compared with Dante's Inferno?

SOPHOMORES.

RHETORIC.

1. What is the difference between Logic and Rhetoric?

2. What an argument "*a priori?*"

3. What is concurrent testimony, and what is its value?

4. What is disbelieving equivalent to?

5. What is included in "Example?"

6. Why do not all men reason alike from the same phenomena?

7. Is common sense a sure guide?

8. What is "Analogy?"

9. What does the parable of the unjust steward teach according to the author's rule?

10. How are matters of opinion established, and how matters of fact?

PREPARATORY DEPARTMENT.

PHYSICAL GEOGRAPHY.

Professor H. J. Fox.

1. Name the great circles.

2. Name the zones and give their latitudes.

3. Give the form and measurements of the earth.

4. How do you prove that it is a sphere?

5. In which Hemisphere is there the most land?

6. Where is the center of the water on the earth?

7. Where is the center of the land?

8. What is the earth's axis?

9. In what order were its parts created?

10. What is Physical Geography?

HISTORY—THIRD FORM.

Professor H. J. Fox.

1. What is History ?
2. To what division of the human race do we belong ?
3. What was the ancient language of India ?
4. Who divided Europe and Asia with the Aryans ?
5. What were the three great divisions of the Semitic Nations ?
6. How did they disperse ?
7. Who were the Celts, and where did they settle ?
8. Teutons ? and slaves ?
9. What great battles did the Greeks fight ?   Who were their generals and historians ?
10. What city became mistress of the world, and how ?

CHEMISTRY, &c.

Professor B. B. BABBITT :

DEAR SIR—In the department of Chemistry, Geology, &c., I have under instruction two classes.

The Seniors use as a text book, Lyell's " Principles of Geology."   The minerals and fossils of the cabinet are studied in connection with this course.

The Junior class in Chemistry have made commendable progress ; as text books we are using Cooke's " Chemical Philosophy," and Eliot & Storer's " Manual of Chemistry."   Blackboard exercises in chemical problems are alternated with the lectures and experiments of the course.

I have also had in charge the Sub-Freshman class in Algebra ; as a class they have done exceedingly well, several of them showing more than average mathematical talent.

The College cabinet, containing several thousand specimens of minerals and fossils, I found last year in dust and disorder.   The work of cleaning, arranging and making a catalogue of the specimens has been continued during spare hours.   Some new specimens have been obtained.

I must again call attention to the dearth of apparatus and material necessary for analyses and scientific research.   The small annual appropriation for the chemical department is insufficient to meet the expense of chemicals consumed, and purchase even one-tenth of the appliances needed to bring this portion of the scientific course up to the full standard of efficiency.

The University has for many years been far behind the times in this respect.   While colleges in the North spend tens of thousands on their laboratories and lecture room appliance, $200 has been our maximum allowance. Even taking into full consideration the poverty of the State this is a " pennywise pound-foolish " policy.

The State University should be a center of information and training in such portions of science as may advance the mineral and agricultural interests of the State. It is difficult to make it so without a better appointed laboratory. Students showing an aptitude for these studies should have an opportunity of pursuing special and advanced courses. With even a few hundred dollars, the foundation may be laid of a school of practical science, which, with the aid of the friends of liberal education, might in time rival those to be found in States where the arts and sciences have reached a higher development.

I append copies of the papers on which the Senior, Junior and Sub-Freshman classes have just been examined.

To attain a mark of 100, a perfect answer to every question was required, and for each inaccuracy or omission a corresponding deduction was made. The marks attained by the great majority have been most creditable.

Respectfully, &c.,

WM. MAIN, Jr.

EXAMINATION QUESTIONS IN GEOLOGY—PROFESSOR MAIN.

Senior Class, February, 1875.

1. Geology has contended against many prejudices, involving :
   First. Prepossessions in regard to the duration of past time.
   Second. Prepossessions regarding the former intensity of aqueous agencies.
   Third. Preconceptions of the former intensity of igneous forces. Discuss these points and show them in their true light.
2. Give an outline of the successive types of animal and vegetable life which have been preserved in the fossil record ?
3. What evidences are there of colder or warmer climates in former ages ?
4. What are the geographical causes of variety of climate ?
5. Explain the astronomical changes influencing climate.
6. What is considered to have been the cause of the last glacial epoch ?
7. Explain the origin of glaciers and the phenomena they present. How is the motion of a glacier accounted for ?
8. Give an account of the structure of the Mississippi delta. What light is afforded us by the study of river deltas ?

QUESTIONS FOR THE EXAMINATION IN CHEMISTRY—PROFESSOR MAIN.

Junior Class, February, 1875.

1. Why are the ideas of atoms and atomic weights necessary forms of thought in explaining chemical phenomena?

2. How was oxygen discovered? How many litres of oxygen can be made from 2.5 kilogrammes of potassic chlorate?

3. Give three ways of decomposing water and liberating hydrogen.

4. Define the terms *atom, molecule, quantivalence, radical, monad, dyad, triad,* giving examples of each.

5. What is ozone? What are its properties? Give the theory of its molecular constitution.

6. Describe the chlorine group of elements.

7. Define and illustrate the meaning of the terms *hydrate, anhydride, acid, base.* Show the formation of such compounds by replacement in one or more molecules of water.

8. Describe the process of manufacturing sulphuric acid. What weight of sulphuric acid can be made from 100 kilogrammes of sulphur?

9. What compounds do nitrogen and oxygen form?

10. What are the properties of phosphorous? Give the formulas of phosphorous anhydride, phosphoric anhydride, phosphoric acid.

11. Give examples of monobasic, bibasic, and tribasic acids; also, of salts of the same.

12. What is "dialysis?" Define the terms "*crystalloid*" and "*colloid.*"

ALGEBRA.

Sub-Freshman Class—February Examination—Professor Main.

1. Divide $6a^4 - a^3b + 2a^2b^3 + 13\ ab^3 + 4b^4$ by $2a^2 - 3ab + 4b^2$.

2. Find the least common multiple of $3a^3b^2\ 9a^2x^2\ 18a^4y^3\ 3a^2y^2$.

3. Find the greatest common divisor of $4ax^2y, 16abx^2, 24acx^2$ and $4ax^2$.

4. Simplify $\dfrac{b-a}{x-b} - \dfrac{a-2b}{x+b} + \dfrac{3x(a-b)}{x^2-b^2}$

5. Multiply $x^2 - x + 1$ by $\dfrac{1}{x^2} + \dfrac{1}{x} + 1$.

6. Divide $\dfrac{4(a_2-ab)}{b(a+b)^2}$ by $\dfrac{6ab}{a^2-b^2}$

7. Divide $\dfrac{a}{a+b} + \dfrac{b}{a-b}$ by $\dfrac{a}{a-b} - \dfrac{b}{a+b}$

8. Simplify $$x + \dfrac{1}{\ \dfrac{1}{1 + \dfrac{x+1}{3-x}}\ }$$

9. $\dfrac{5x-1}{7} + \dfrac{9x-5}{11} = \dfrac{9x-7}{5}$

Find the value of x.

10. $\dfrac{x-3}{4} - \dfrac{2x-5}{6} = 41 \dfrac{}{60} + \dfrac{3x-8}{5} - \dfrac{5x+6}{15}$

Find the value of x.

12. Given $\dfrac{x-3}{4} - \dfrac{2x-5}{6} = \dfrac{41}{60} + \dfrac{3x-8}{5} - \dfrac{5x+6}{15}$ Find the value of x.

11. Why do like signs in multiplication give a positive product and unlike signs a negative?

12. Multiply $3a\frac{1}{3}b^m - 6x^2y\frac{a}{b}$ by $2a\frac{1}{4}b^2 - 3x\frac{1}{2}y^3$

13. Write $x^{\frac{1}{5}},\ a^{\frac{2}{3}},\ z^{\frac{7}{8}},\ z^{\frac{3}{5}}$ in the other form.

UNIVERSITY OF SOUTH CAROLINA,

COLUMBIA, S. C., February 20, 1875.

Rev. B. B. BABBITT, *Chairman of the Faculty:*

DEAR SIR—In response to the resolution passed by the House of Representatives day before yesterday, I respectfully furnish, through you, the present report.

The following is a statement of the studies pursued under my instruction during the past twelve months:

The Class of 1876 (or Junior Class) has recited, in Latin, the whole of Cicero's Treatise on Old Age, and Terence's Comedy of the Self-Tormentor, and seventeen sections of Tacitus' Life of Agricola; in Greek, the whole of Demosthenes' Oration on the Crown.

The Class of 1877 (or Sophomore Class) has recited, in Latin, nine epodes and eleven satires of Horace, the third and half the fourth book of Quintus Curtius' Life of Alexander the Great, and part of Cicero's Treatise on Old Age; in Greek, three hundred lines of the Iliad, fifty-seven sections of Herodotus, nearly one-half of the Acts of the Apostles, and all of Sophocles' Tragedy of King Oedipus. This class has taken almost daily lessons in Hadley's Greek Grammar and Allen's Latin Grammar.

The Class of 1878 (or Freshman Class) has recited, in Latin, in Cæsar, Cicero and Livy, (in Cicero and Virgil to Professor Greener also ;) in Greek, the whole of Harkness' First Greek Book, in Xenophon's Expedition of Cyrus, and eight hundred lines in the Iliad. They have recited also in Hadley's Greek, and Harkness' Latin Grammar.

One special student has recited in Hebrew Grammar and the Epistle to the Romans.

In the reported studies of the present Freshman Class, will be found some of a very elementary character. These belong to the time before the class had entered upon their quadrennial college course. A similar class has recently begun to recite to me in Greek, hoping to be admitted as Freshmen at the beginning of the next Academic year. The Trustees have prohibited the formation of Sub-Freshman classes after this session, the proper place for preparatory students being evidently in the Preparatory School. There may, however, still be a necessity for elementary instruction in the languages, for students in the Modern Course who wish to be transferred to the Classical.

For copies of what was required in Latin and Greek of the Sophomores and Freshmen, at the late semi-annual examination, I refer to the accompanying documents, marked A and B.

Your obedient servant,

FISK P. BREWER,
Professor of Ancient Languages and Literature.

A.—EXAMINATION IN GREEK.—February 9, 1875.

The Sophomore examination was on nine lines of the Oedipus, with questions on the moods and participles. The Freshmen were examined on four lines of the Iliad, with Etymology, Inflection and Prosody. They were also called upon to write, from memory, the translation of another passage. The examination papers themselves, as well as those of the Sub-Freshman Class, are omitted for want of Greek type.

B.—EXAMINATION IN LATIN.—February 10, 1875.

SOPHOMORES.

1. Translate—Volumus sane, nisi molestum est, Cato, tamquam longam aliquam viam confeceris quam nobis quoque ingrediundum sit, istuc quo pervenisti videre quale sit.

2. Translate—Ut enim adulescentibus bona indole praeditis sapientes senes delectantur, leviorque fit senectus eorum qui a juventute coluntur et diliguntur, sic adulescentes senum praeceptis gaudent, quibus ad virtutum studia ducuntur.

3. What would be the more common phrase for *quam ingrediundum sit ?*

4. What is the construction of *molestum,* of *nobis,* of *istuc,* of *adulescentibus ?*

5. What are the four objections against which Cato defends old age ?

6. Which of them is he replying to in the second passage quoted above ?

7. What occasion does he have for referring to Milo ?

8. In what connection is Plato named ?

9. What book did Cato write ?

10. What Latin poets does Cato quote in " de Senectute "?

11. State the substance of the introduction to the " de Senectute."

1. Translate—Tarquinius Sextus, qui Romae relictus fuerat, ut ignarus responsi expersque imperii, esset, rem summa ope taceri jubent : ipsi inter se, uter prior, cum Romam redissent, matri osculum daret, sorti permittunt. Brutus, alio ratus spectare Pythicam vocem, velut si prolapsus cecidisset, terram osculo contigit, scilicet, quod ea communis mater omnium mortalium esset. Reditum inde Romam, ubi adversus Rutulos bellum summa vi parabatur.

2. Give the construction of *Tarquinius* and *imperii.*

3. What does *ut* connect ?

4. Give the reason for the mood of *esset, daret,* and *esset.*

5. Parse *reditum.*

6. To what place does *inde* refer ?

7. Who was the last king of Rome ?

8. Give the names of all the kings in regular order.

9. What was the motive for war against the Rutuli ?

10. What was their chief city ?

MENTAL AND MORAL SCIENCE, &c.

UNIVERSITY OF SOUTH CAROLINA,
COLUMBIA, February 18, 1875.

Rev. B. B. BABBITT, A. M., *Chairman of the Faculty:*

In accordance with the custom of the University, and in obedience to the resolution of the General Assembly communicated to you, I have the honor to report my department as in an excellent condition during the past collegiate year, in consequence of the ability and earnest character of the members of the Senior and Junior classes, more than by reason of the number in my particular school.

In the first term of 1873-4, I heard recitations from the Senior Class, in *Hamilton's Metaphysics* three times per week; in *Jevons' Logic* once a week, and at the end of the term, two recitations per week in *Porter's Intellectual Science.*

At that time, we had no Senior Class. I assisted, however, as I have since my connection with the University, in the Preparatory School, then under the able direction of the Rev. Henry J. Fox, A. M., D. D. I had the Sub-Freshman Class in Latin, and they recited five times per week in the *Orations of Cicero* and, the *Æneid of Virgil.* They are all members at present of the Freshman Classical Class in the Academic Department. In addition, I had an advanced class in English Grammar from the Preparatory School four times per week.

While remaining at the University during the summer months, I tutored certain members of the Preparatory School, who were ambitious to advance. They are now in the Sub-Freshman Class.

For the present term, my duties have been divided as follows:

SENIOR CLASS.

1. *Porter's Intellectual Science,* twice per week.
2. *Jevons' Logic,* once a week.
3. *Townsend's Analysis of the Constitution of the United States,* once a week. All these have been completed, with the exception of the *Constitution,* the last part of which, together with a study of *Constitutional Law* or *International Law,* has been reserved for the present term.

JUNIOR CLASS.

1. This class has recited in :—
2. *Bowen's Metaphysics & Ethics,* three times per week.
3. *Peabody's Moral Philosophy,* once a week.
4. *Stewart's Philosophy of the Human Mind* was used temporarily; but owing to a difficulty in procuring this text book, it was given up for the above named. The others, with the exception of the *Ethics,* have

been completed in a creditable manner, and excellent examinations passed upon them.

In common with other members of the Faculty, I have assisted in the very important work of advancing the Sub-Freshman class. This has been at once a light duty and a source of gratification, performed, it is true, at an expense of leisure for other studies and more attention to the advanced classes but one that has amply recompensed me in the progress of the students. I invited into this class those members of the Freshman Modern, and such students of the Preparatory School, as I deemed fitted. They have recited five times per week, for the most part, in Harkness' Latin Reader and Grammar and since November five times per week in Harkness' First Book in Greek. Not only the deep interest of the students and their friendly rivalry; but the daily recitations and the actual work done in the examinations give sufficient, indubitable evidence of the good already accomplished by the organization of this class. These young men, by their studious habits and gentlemanly behavior, have proved themselves worthy of the bounty of the State, and justify the judgment of the State Board of Examiners, who preferred to retain them here and instruct them in the University rather than to dismiss them to the several Counties where absolutely no opportunity for higher instruction lay open to them. From this class of nearly forty members, twenty attained an average of seventy per cent. or over in Latin. In Greek, with thirty-two members twenty-two attained seventy per cent. or over, and ten reached eighty-five per cent. or over. Whether the examinations were rigid or not may be judged from the questions asked, copies of which are enclosed.

A. All the examination papers in my department.

B. The monthly averages of the students, the marks obtained in the examination, and the general averages for the past term.

I am, very respectfully,

RICHARD T. GREENER,
Professor, Mental and Moral Philosophy, &c.

SEMI-ANNUAL EXAMINATION, UNIVERSITY OF SOUTH CAROLINA, FEBRUARY 13, 1875.

SENIOR CLASS.

Professor R. T. Greener.

PORTER'S ELEMENTS OF INTELLECTUAL SCIENCE.

1. Analyze Sense-Perception. Give the theories of Democritus, Plato, Aristotle, Malebranche, Berkeley and Kant on this subject.

2. Explain the Primary and Secondary Laws of the Association of Ideas.

3. What elements are essential to an act of Memory? Name the different varieties of Memory?

4. Show how the growth and culture of the Imagination is possible?

5. How would you distinguish Reasoning from Judgment proper? What two kinds of Reasoning? Explain each. Give Campbell's and J. Stuart Mill's criticism on the form of the Syllogism. Give an example from scientific discovery to illustrate Inductive Reasoning.

6. Give other names for the Intuitions or Categories, and tell how they are divided? What is a Principle, and what are the limitations of Sense-Perception?

7. Define the Law of Causation. Is acquiesence in this an early or later intellectual growth? Give Comte's opinion. What theories with regard to Causation were held by Locke, Hamilton and Mill?

8. Define Efficient Cause, Final Cause? What two facts can you state with regard to the relation of these? Illustrate Design or Final Cause.

9. Explain the terms Finite, Conditioned, Infinite, Absolute, as applied in Psychology. Under which would you place Spinoza's *Omnis determinatio est negatio?*

10. What are Herbert Spencer's objections to Hamilton's and Mansel's Unknowableness of the Infinite? How is the Finite Universe, according to President Porter, Infinite according to our knowledge, and why must he assume the Absolute both to exist and be unknowable?

SENIOR CLASS.

Prof. Greener.

JEVONS' LOGIC.

1. Name the various kinds of terms and state wherein they may be ambiguous.

2. Name the following Conversions:—

A to I, I to I, E to E, O, and A.

3. Give Descartes' four rules of method.

Give Pascal's five rules of method.

4. What are the Primary Laws of Thought?

What two canons of the Syllogism are usually added to these?

5. Give the eight rules for the Syllogism.

Name the number of moods; the valid ones.

If X=major term, Y=middle term, and Z=minor term, show how the four figures of the Syllogism are developed from this. For what purpose is each figure best suited?

6. How does Aristotle divide the Fallacies?

Name the Semi-logical fallacies. Under what classes would you place the following:—

1. $\begin{cases} \text{Three and two are two numbers.} \\ \text{Three and two are five.} \\ \therefore \text{ Five is two numbers.} \end{cases}$ 2. $\begin{cases} \text{Tu es qui es.} \\ \text{Quies est requies.} \\ \text{Ergo, tu es Requies.} \end{cases}$

3. $\{$ B is C, A is B $\therefore$ A is C.

7. Define the Quantification of the Predicate.

What, in brief, was Mr. Boole's attempt in Logic, and what led to his method?

8. Define Method in Discovery and Method in Instruction. To what are these analogous in Metaphysics? Explain the use of the expressions *a priori* and *a posteriori*.

9. What are Perfect and Imperfect Induction?

"Every science and every question in science is first a matter of fact only, then a matter of quantity, and by degrees becomes more and more precisely quantitative."

What inquiries arise from this with regard to every question of Quantitative Induction?

10. Define and illustrate Classification and Abstraction.

BOWEN'S METAPHYSICS AND ETHICS.

JUNIOR CLASS.

Prof. Greener.

1. State the "logic" of Metaphysical and Physical inquiry.

2. Give the error and results of the teaching of the Schoolmen.

3. What kind of a question is that of the existence of an external world?

4. Develop the idea of Self or personal existence; Hume, Leibnitz, the Ancients.

5. State the Law of Causation; distinguish it from mere Succession; what are General Laws, Laws of Nature? From whence do we derive the idea of Cause?

6. Show the difference between Fatalism and Free-will. Give Fichte's exposition of the former. What are *Natura Naturans* and *Natura Naturata?* Give Mill's idea of Causation.

7. Give the argument for the Immediate Agency of the Deity. What is Anthropomorphism and the objection to it.

8. Show how Universal Scepticism cures itself; analyze the doctrine of Chance, and state the Argument from Design.

9. Give the relation of Theology to the Physical Sciences.

10. What six doctrines are there to account for the motions and other phenomena of the material universe?

MORAL PHILOSOPHY—PEABODY.

JUNIOR CLASS.

Prof. Greener.

1. Name the Desires and explain how they differ from the Appetites.

2. Discuss the ground of Right.

3. Show how Observation, Experience and Tradition are sources of Knowledge.

4. What limitations are there with regard to our Right to Liberty and Property ?

5. What are our duties in the attainment of knowledge ?

6. What is Casuistry ; its original application ; its more general signification now ? Give examples.

7. Describe briefly the Epicurean and the Peripatetic schools of Ethics.

8. What relation does Cicero bear to the Grecian Ethics ?

9. Give, in brief, the Ethical systems of Paley and Bentham.

10. What was Malebranche's definition of Virtue? Illustrate. State the idea of the Pantheistic School of virtue.

PRIVATE EXAMINATION IN LATIN,

DECEMBER 21st, 1874.

SUB-FRESHMAN.

Prof. Greener.

1. Give the *mood, tense, person* and *voice* of :
   Laudetur ; fugatæ sunt,
   Monear, terreret, regendum, scribat,
   Sciet, sequitur, capientur and miramur.

2. *Translate* and give the *rules* for the *cases* of the underscored words :

I. Labor *omnia* vincit. 2. Fortuna bella *artem victos* docet. 3. Appius Claudius cæcus *annos multos* fuit. 4. Se obtulit *omnia* Mercurio similis *vocemque coloremque*. 5. Non *scholæ* sed *vitæ* discimus. 6. Leges omnium salutem singulorum saluti anteponunt. 7. Hic *mihi* Furius pacis commoda commemorat. 8. Legiones duas *castris præsidio* reliquit. 9. Crescit amor *nummi*. 10. Fuit peritus *belli*. 11. Cæsar, *victis hostibus*, Romam rediit. 12. Doctrina, propter *se*, expetenda est. 13. *Jove* nate, Hercules, salve! 14. Nihil est veritatis *luce* dulcius. 15. Nemo fit *casu* doctus. 16. Multis *duce* opus est. 17. Solus potitus est *imperio*. 18. Nemo puerorum omnibus *horis* sapit. 19. Nihil studentibus sine magno *labore* dedit. 20. In amnem ruerunt et sub *ipsa mœnia* progressi sunt.

3. Give the *principal parts* of: Sum, duco, disco, habeo, facio, juvo, utor, fugo, trajicio and gaudeo.

4. Tell from what the following are *compounded:*

Interfecerunt, percurrit, prætervectus, edoctus, rediit, alloquitur, reipublicæ, infantibus, constituit and egregiam.

5. Mark the *quantity* of the *penults* in:

Cæsaris, Capua, Antiochia, Timoleon, Chersonesus, alius, Miltiades, Iberus, Antiochus, philosophus.

6. What is a Deponent verb? Into how many parts is the *Periphrastic conjugation* divided? What does each form express? Give an example of each.

7. What are *ve, que, ne* called when appended to words? What are the endings of Masculine, Feminine and Neuter nouns of the III Dec.?

8. What *Prepositions* are followed by the *Accusative?*

9. What *Prepositions* are followed by the *Ablative?*

10. Give a *Synopsis* of *Capio* in the *Present, Indicative,* and *Subjunctive, Active,* with *Imperative, Participles,* &c.

MODERN FRESHMAN, SUB-FRESHMAN AND PREPARATORY STUDENTS.

Semi-Annual Examination, February, 1875.

LATIN.

Prof. Greener.

Translate:

1. *Hoc facinus* rex *miratur.*
2. *Pacem te poscimus.*
3. Dionysius *navigabat Syracusas.*
4. Hannibal *femur* ictus *cecidit.*

5. Milites non *mulieribus,* non *infantibus pepercerunt.*

6. Tu virtutem *praefer divitiis.*

7. *Trojæ* huic *loco* nomen est.

8. Ego spem *pretio* non *emo.*

9. Solis *occasu* suas copias Ariovistus in *castra reduxit.*

10. *Scipione duce, ponte facto, superaverunt* Ticinum flumen.

11. Si te *rogavero aliquid,* non *respondebis ?*

12. Philosophia *nos docuit,* ut *nosmet* ipsos nosceremus.

13. *Equidem vellem,* ut *redires.*

14. Ne quis, tanquam parva, *fastidiat* grammaticæ elementa.

15. Timoleon *oravit* omnes, *ne* id *facerent.*

16. Lex brevis est, *quo* facilius ab *imperitis teneatur.*

17. *Oderint,* dum *metuant.* Licet ipsa vitium *sit.*

18. Quam magnum *vectigal sit* parsimonia !

19. *Quid est, cur non* orator de rebus iis eloquentissime *dicat,* quas *cognorit ?*

20. In Hortensio memoria *tanta* fuit, ut, quæ secum *commentatus esset,* ea verbis iisdem *redderet,* quibus *cogitavisset.*

21. Divico ita cum Cæsare egit, si pacem populus Romanus cum *Helvetiis faceret,* in eam partem *ituros* Helvetios, ubi eos Cæsar esse voluisset ; *sin* bello persequi *perseveraret, reminisceretur* pristinæ *virtutis* Helvetiorum.

22. Cura, ut *quam primum venias.*

23. Cato esse quam *videri* doctus *malebat.*

24. Consul *placandis diis* dat operam.

25. Pacem *petitum* legatum Romam *mittunt.*

26. Dionysius *Corinthi* expulsus *Syracusis* pueros *docebat.*

27. Jus *sua sponte* est *expetendum.*

1. Parse all the italicised nouns and give the rules for the cases.

2. Parse all the italicised verbs. Give their principal parts, voice mood, tense, number and person. State why they are in the subjunctive mood, if they are. When they are compounded, give the elements. What is omitted with *ituros?* composition of *sin ?*

3. What is *met* in *nosmet?* composition of *Equidem ?* full form for *cognorit ?* the correlatives of *tanta ? nos ?* What kind of clauses are *ut* , *nosceremus? ut* , *redires? ne* , *facerent ?* Explain *quam primum.*

4. Give colloquial English for *Quid est, cur non.* Give the English of sentence 21, in the *oratio directa.*

5. Where were Syracuse, Corinth, Ticinus, Rome, Troy ?

The Sub-Freshman Class was also examined in Harkness' First Book in Greek, on the translation, paradigms and the Active and Middle Voices of Bouleuo. The following questions were also asked :

4. What does the middle voice in Greek denote ?

What is it similar to in Latin and French ?

How many voices are there ?

Explain the Optative mood. Show its relation to the English Potential, the Latin Subjunctive.

What does the Aorist tense denote ?

How does it resemble, if at all, the Imperfect ?

What tenses are necessary, in giving the principal parts of a verb in Greek ?

B 1.

SENIORS.	October.	November.	December.	January.	Examination.	Total.
Metaphysics, Logic, Constitution of United States.						
Babbitt, C. J.	70	72	68	79	95	84
Stewart, T. Mc	61	65	47	55	75	66
Fox, H.	70	97				84
JUNIORS.						
Metaphysics, Moral Philosophy.						
Dart	65	79	88	80	85	82
Morris	68	63	94	91	X	79
Mishow	60	76	X	X	X	68
Townsend	70	80	83	86	90	85

GREEK.	Department.	November.	December.	January.	Examination.	Total.
Avery	P.	60	73	67	83	69
Cooper	P.	72	58	60	X	63
Clinton	S. F.	78	81	60	83	77
Durham	S. F.	80	75	X	50	68
Edwards	P.	X	X	43	50	47
Goosley	S. F.	55	52	55	50	53
Hampton	P.	80	76	75	75	77
Hart	S. F.	78	76	79	87	79
Henderson	S. F.	58	95	97	95	92
Holland	S. F.	80	88	55	75	78
Johnston	S. F.	80	90	94	90	91
Kershaw	S. F.	80	92	91	92	91
LaVall	P.	68	75	60	X	68
Lee	S. F.	60	58	43	50	25
McCoy	S. F.	90	96	92	94	93
McKinlay	M. F.	72	80	60	88	75
Murray	S. F.	90	93	88	90	91
Oliver	S. F.	80	82	88	89	83
Purcell	M. F.	75	80	70	82	77
Roberts	M. F.	85	86	87	88	86
Scott	M. F.	79	80	70	85	79
Shippen	M. F.	95	83	65	85	78
Shrewsbury	M. F.	85	90	93	93	89
Sinclair	S. F.	80	86	80	88	84
Smith	S. F.	55	57	60	60	57
Stewart	M. F.	80	82	74	86	81
Wallace	P.	85	97	80	92	89
Whittaker	S. F.	90	98	100	95	95
Williams, G. D.	M. F.	78	81	60	75	76
Williams, G. L.	S. F.	85	82	74	86	85
Young	S. F.	75	83	55	50	70

MARKS FOR THE SECOND TERM (1874–75) IN METAPHYSICS, MORAL PHILOSOPHY, CONSTITUTION, LOGIC, GREEK AND LATIN — *Professor Richard T. Greener.*—Seniors, S. Juniors, J. Modern Freshmen, M. F. Sub-Freshmen, S. F. Preparatory School, P. X, left, absent during that time, or not present at the examination.

B 2.

LATIN.	OCTOBER.	NOVEMBER.	DECEMBER.	JANUARY.	EXAMINATION.	TOTAL.	DEPARTMENT.
Agnew	70	75	63	77	90	71	P.
Allen	65	68	56	55	50	61	M. F.
Avery	55	60	49	75	87	60	P.
Cooper	58	70	57	80	X	66	P.
Davis	60	68	52	67	75	62	M. F.
Durham	73	75	57	60	60	66	S. F.
Fillebrown	80	80	80	95	93	84	S. F.
Fox, Irving	80	75	78	87	93	80	P.
Fox, Clarence	75	70	73	98	97	79	S. F.
Hampton	60	60	60	78	84	65	P.
Hart	68	70	59	73	85	68	S. F.
Henderson	80	80	85	98	97	66	S. F.
Holland	76	77	60	85	87	75	S. F.
LaVall	80	80	61	80	87	75	P.
Lee	60	62	61	50	50	58	S. F.
McCoy	75	87	88	97	96	87	S. F.
McKinlay	62	65	66	85	95	70	M. F.
McLaurin	70	75	70	84	92	75	M. F.
Oliver	69	72	61	87	90	72	S. F.
Purcell	65	71	69	82	86	72	M. F.
Roberts	64	74	77	89	93	76	M. F.
Scott	70	73	58	73	85	69	M. F.
Seay	75	77	X	X	X	76	M. F.
Shippen	64	66	57	70	80	64	M. F.
Shrewsbury	67	88	82	99	98	84	M. F.
Simmons	52	52	60	50	50	54	S. F.
Sinclair	75	77	64	89	94	76	S. F.
Smith, A. S.	60	50	23	57	60	48	S. F.
Smith, O. L. W.	35	50	40	57	60	51	M. F.
Stewart	80	82	74	83	91	80	M. F.
Wallace	80	86	84	98	97	87	P.
Williams, G. D.	65	70	75	60	60	68	M. F.
Williams, G. L.	80	80	62	82	90	76	S. F.
*Clinton	...	...	...	...	76	76	S. F.
*Durant	...	...	...	...	50	50	S. F.
*Edwards	...	...	...	...	50	50	P.
*Johnston	...	...	...	...	75	75	S. F.
*Kershaw	...	...	...	...	77	77	S. F.
*McMorris	...	...	...	...	60	60	S. F.
*Murray	...	...	...	...	75	75	S. F.
*Simkins	...	...	...	...	76	76	S. F.
*Whittaker	...	...	...	...	60	60	S. F.
*Young	...	...	...	...	50	50	S. F.

*These scholars, during the months of October, November, and December, were in a lower division; but gained the above marks by passing the same examination with the others at the end of the term.

MODERN LANGUAGES, &c.

To the Chairman of the Faculty of the University of South Carolina:

SIR—In response to your request for a report of the state of my Department in the University, I have to say that I entered upon my duties as Professor of Modern Languages on the first day of the present month. This was one week preceding the semi-annual examination, and in view of the change of Professors at this juncture it was thought advisable by the Faculty to omit the intermediate examination of the classes in my Department. I have, therefore, no report of examinations to present.

On assuming the duties of my Department I found students pursuing the study of French and German in the Senior, Junior, Sophomore and Freshman classes, together with two from the Preparatory School and two special students. The number of Seniors in my Department is 2; of Juniors, 3; of Sophomores, 1; and of Freshmen, 13. The whole number reciting is 23.

The Seniors recite four times a week; the Juniors four times; the Sophomore and Freshman classes, together, five times. The Sophomores, in Greek, also recite to me four times a week.

I think the most of these students evince an earnest desire to make progress in their studies. I am happily impressed with the serious, orderly and gentlemanly bearing of the students in the recitation room, in which respect, I am disposed to assert, they are not surpassed by the students of any college in the land.

Respectfully submitted.

E. B. OTHEMAN,
Professor of Modern Languages, University of South Carolina.
College Campus, February 22, 1875.

PHYSIOLOGY AND MATERIA MEDICA.

UNIVERSITY OF SOUTH CAROLINA,
COLUMBIA, S. C., February, 1875.

Rev. B. B. BABBITT, A. M., *Chairman of Faculty U. S. C.:*

DEAR SIR—I herewith transmit a report of the progress of the classes in Physiology and Mat. Medica, under my charge for the term ending February 1, 1875. Although the classes, under existing circumstances, have been small, the members have been generally regular in attendance and in their recitations. Only one member of the classes presented himself for the intermediate examination, viz: James A. Beattie.

I take pleasure in sending in the result of his examinations.

In Physiology.. 87–100
In Mat. Medica... 83–100

Very respectfully,

JOHN LYNCH,
Prof. Physiology and Mat. Med., U. S. C.

LAW.

OFFICE OF MESSRS. MELTON & CLARK,
ATTORNEYS-AT-LAW,
COLUMBIA, S. C., February 15, 1875.

Prof. BABBITT, *Chairman of Faculty University of So.*

Carolina:

SIR—I respectfully report that on Tuesday, the 9th instant, the Intermediate Examination of the Law Class was had, upon written questions and answers, with the following result:

H. A. Fox	97
H. B. Johnson	94
J. H. Stuart	97
T. McCants Stewart	60

These are the only members of the class who have submitted to the daily examinations. The average stand of Mr. T. McCants Stewart has been better than that exhibited by his answers to the Examination Paper.

Respectfully your most obedient,

C. D. MELTON,
Law Professor.

REPORT OF SECRETARY AND LIBRARIAN.

UNIVERSITY OF SOUTH CAROLINA,
COLUMBIA, February 23, 1875.

Rev. BENJAMIN B. BABBITT, A. M., *Chairman of the Faculty:*

DEAR SIR—In reply to your request, I respectfully state that the following named students have registered in the University, since the commencement of the term, October, 1874, viz:

LAW SCHOOL.

1. Barnett B. Goins .... October 2, 1874, resigned.
2. Edgar Caypless ....October 8, 1874, resigned.
3. Joseph H. Stuart ....October 2, 1874.
4. C. W. Cummings ....October 7, 1873, re-entered.
5. Harry A. Fox ....May 5, 1874.
6. E. W. Everson ....October 5, 1874.
7. F. L. Cardozo ....October 7, 1874.

8. Thomas M. Canton..October 7, 1874.
9. Richard T. Greener..October 7, 1874.
10. Gil Dixon Fox...October 7, 1874.
11. John Wingate...October 9, 1874.
12. Walter R. Jones.............................October 2, 1874, re-entered.
13. Henry B. Johnson..October 10, 1874.
14. James O. Ladd..October 12, 1874.
15. Paul J. Mishow..November 24, 1874.
16. L. Cain...................................October 30, 1873, re-entered.
17. Mortimer A. Warren..October 7, 1874·

SCHOOL OF MEDICINE.

1. H. E. Hayne.....................................October 7, 1873, re-entered.
2. Charles N. Hunter.......................... ......October 2, 1874, resigned.
3. James A. Beattie........................... ......October 7, 1873, re-entered.
4. M. J. O'Dowd...................................... ....November 2, 1874.

SENIORS.

1. Charles J. Babbitt..October 7, 1873.
2. T. McCants Stewart...January 7, 1874.

JUNIORS.

1. A. G. Townsend...January 7, 1874.
2. J. M. Morris... ....January 5, 1874.
3. Wm. M. Dart............................ ....January, 5, 1874.
4. Paul J. Mishow..........................January 1, 1874, entered in law.

SOPHOMORES.

1. Olin T. Cummings..October 7, 1874.
2. Cornelius C. Scott..January 5, 1874.
3. E. M. Babbitt...October 7, 1873.
4. Lester D. Puckett, (modern).................................April 1, 1874.
5. T. A. McLean...October 5, 1874.

FRESHMEN.

1. C. C. McKinney...October 5, 1874.
2. Thaddeus Saltus..October 18, 1873.
3. Joseph M. O'Hear..February 16, 1874.
4. T. R. Evans...... ....October 5, 1874.
5. W. H. Shrewsbury..... ....October 5, 1874.
6. I. Nunez Cardozo... October 5, 1874.

7. Owen L. W. Smith..April 1, 1874.
8. Whitefield McKinlay...................................... October 5, 1874.
9. G. W. Dickson...October 5, 1874.
10. N. C. Davis...April 1, 1875.
11. T. Frank P. Roberts.......................................October 5, 1874.
12. J. L. Purcell...October 5, 1874.
13. W. J. Williams................................. ....April 1, 1874.
14. Philip W. Shippen...October 5, 1874.
15. Edward J. Stewart...April 1, 1874.
16. Milton McLauren..April 1, 1874.
17. C. R. Parmele...October 5, 1874.
18. J. F. Lay..April 1, 1874.
19. N. H. Middleton...April 1, 1874.
20. J. H. Seay...April 1, 1874.
21. Lewis C. Scott...October 2, 1874.
22. Milton B. Lawrence.......................................December 11, 1873.
23. G. D. Williams.................... ....April 1, 1874.
24. John L. Allen...October 2, 1874.
25. C. D. Stewart..October 21, 1874.
26. J. G. Varn...November 21, 1874.
27. L. O'B. Posey..November 21, 1874.
28. Peter V. Hazel.............................. ....November 21, 1874.
29. John L. Dart.. ....February 12, 1875.

SUB FRESHMEN.

1. Albert Gooseley.............. ....October 13, 1874.
2. H. L. Fillebrown.....................................November 21, 1874.
3. Clarence W. Fox.......................................November 21, 1874.
4. Benjamin Simmons, Jr.............................November 28, 1874.
5. A. H. Durant...November 21, 1874.
6. H. R. Pinckney.......................................February 15, 1875.
7. Zebulon W. McMorris....................................October 5, 1874.
8. George E. Hart..April 1, 1874.
9. J. J. Durham...October 5, 1874.
10. J. A. Simkins....................................... .....October 2, 1874.
11. George W. Murray...October 5, 1874.
12. John L. Williams..October 5, 1874.
13. J. C. Whittaker...October 5, 1874.
14. K. M. Young........................ ....October 5, 1874.
15. H. B. Kershaw................................ ....October 5, 1874.
16. Julius J. Holland..October 5, 1874.
17. S. H. McCoy..October 5, 1874.

18 J. L. Oliver...October 5, 1874.
19. F. H. Henderson..October 5, 1874.
20. W. A. Sinclair..October 5, 1874.
21. Robert O. Lee ....October 5, 1874.
22. G. W. C. Clinton...October 5, 1874.
23. James H. Johnston.......................................October 5, 1874.
54. A. S. Smith........... ....April 1, 1874.

SPECIAL COURSE.

1. F. A. Cummings...October 8, 1874.
2. S. A. Camp ....October 8, 1874.

SUMMARY.

Law School................ 17
Medical School.. 4
Senior.. 2
Junior...... 4
Sophomores... 5
Freshman 29
Sub-Freshman 24
Special Course... 2
Preparatory School...79
                                                                    ——
Total...166

Very respectfully,

ERASTUS W. EVERSON,

Secretary of the Faculty.

APPENDIX IV.

PREPARATORY SCHOOL.

Rev. B. B. BABBITT, *Chairman of the Faculty of the University of South Carolina :*

SIR—I have the honor to transmit herewith my report of the Preparatory School of the University since my connection with it.

On October 13, 1874, Hon. J. K. Jillson temporarily appointed me Assistant Principal, or Head Master of the School, and I assumed my duties on the 14th; on the 12th of December I was elected Principal by the Board of Trustees.

October 14 there were on the roll fifty-five names, distributed in classes as follows: First Form, 32; Second Form, 14; Third Form, 9. Since that time 2·from the Third and 1 from the Second Forms have been admitted to the Sub-Freshman Class of the University; eight have been advanced from the Second to the Third Form; four have been admitted, upon examination, to the Second Form, and nine have been advanced from the First Form; twelve have been admitted to the First Form, and we have, at present, ten special students conditioned for the First Form. I have to record the death of one of the students of the Second Form, which occurred October 20, 1874; two have left the School; so that at present there are seventy-three in attendance, distributed as follows: First Form, (including ten conditioned,) 41; Second Form, 18; Third Form, 14.

SUMMARY.

Number in attendance, October 14............................. 55
Admitted since... 24
                                                            ——
　　Total... 79

Entered University.. 3
Left School... 2
Death... 1
                                                            ——
　　Total... 6
                                                            ——
　　Balance... 73

The course of study as printed in the last annual catalogue of the University, although possessing, in itself, many good qualities, is, to my mind, entirely unpractical, and unfit for the purpose designed.

The object of the Preparatory School being to fit students to enter the University, they should manifestly pursue such a course of study as will accomplish the purpose, and not an entirely different and independent one. My design is, therefore, to adopt such a course that the student, having completed it, will be entitled to enter the Freshman Class of the University without further examination.

The course contemplates four years in completing, which I deem absolutely necessary, at least for the present; the very limited opportunities offered throughout the State, and, in many cases, the superficial manner of teaching, make it imperative that the course in this department should be so arranged as to supply these deficiencies. To Mr. Harry A. Fox, my efficient assistant, I wish to express my obligation, for his uniform and hearty co-operation in all my efforts to promote the welfare of the school.

I append a copy of the roll of each Form, together with copies of the examination questions, and the per cent. attained by each student for the term just closed.

Yours, very respectfully,

WM. H. JACKSON,

Principal Preparatory School.

First Form.

Standing.	Name.	Age.	Per Cent.
1	Taylor..	16	95
2	Mishaw...	16	84
3	H. Mobley...	13	82
4	Mitchell..	16	80
5	Avery...	13	79
6	Spellman..	13	79
7	Lee..	10	78
8	Steele..	13	76
9	Williams..	15	72
10	Gibbs...	13	71
11	Parker..	19	69
12	N. E. Lewis...	13	69
13	J. Thomas...	14	68
14	Edmonston..	18	68
15	H. E. Lewis...	15	67
16	Pinckney..	11	65
17	J. Mobley...	15	65
18	Washington..	13	57
19	Simmons...	20	57
20	Sightler..	14	57
21	Edwards..	14	56
22	Brawley..	17	55
23	Allen..	16	55
24	Camp...	18	53
25	Johnson..	12	53
26	Major...	14	53
27	Harris...	16	50
28	Martin..	14	50
29	Gourdion..	16	50
30	Tardiff..	13	
31	O'Harra..	14	
32	O'Sullivan*..	12	

SPECIAL STUDENTS.

1	Samuels..	18	44
2	McMorris..	16	37
3	Scott..	10	37
4	Calvo...	16	
5	Stannard...	19	
6	Clinton...	14	
7	Jordan..	18	
8	Lomax..	18	
9	Jones...	16	
10	Brown..	18	

*Entered school since examination.

Second Form.

Standing.	Name.	Age.	Per Cent.
1	Oliver, P.	14 82	7–10
2	Smith, W. B.	15 76	3–5
3	Douglass, E. J.	20 75	3–5
4	Kennedy, Jno.	14 75	1–10
5	Reese, H. O.	16 75	
6	Buchar, Jno.	14 73	
7	LaRoche, Jas. S.	19 72	2–5
8	Ramsay, W. W.	15 72	2–5
9	Rainey	18 68	
10	Bradley, C. S.	20 67	4–5
11	Smith, W. T.	17 66	
12	Stewart, R. A.	13 64	3–5
13	Raiford	16 63	2–5
14	Smith, S.	20 62	3–5
15	Williams, Manson, Jr.	18 56	3–5
16	Jones, Lawrence	21 49	4–5
17	Campbell, R. P.	17 45	
18	Williams, J. F.	23 35½	
19	Hayne, J. B.*	15	

*Entered school since examination.

Third Form.

Standing.	Name.	Age.	Per Cent.
1	Wallace, J. E.	15 87	3–4
2	Fox, I. P.	14 80	5–6
3	Cummings, F. A.	18 79	17–25
4	Agnew, Holmes.	12 75	1–2
5	Shelton, N. S.	20 71	
5	Hampton, R. P.	19 70	
7	Lavall, W. A.	15 67	2–7
8	Clinton, Lewis.	17 60	1–6
9	Edwards, J. A.	18 59	61–100
10	Avery, R.	15 68	31–50
11	Williams, A. P.	19 58	1–5
12	Rafra, J. T.	19 57	43–50
13	Nance, B. W.	17 52	1–2
14	Penn, R. S.	20 52	

GRAMMAR—THIRD FORM.

Wm. H. Jackson.

1. What is the distinction between General Grammar and English Grammar? Into how many parts is English Grammar divided? Define each.

2. Give the rules for the use of Capital letters.

3. How many, and what are the parts of Speech? Define each.

4. Into how many classes are Nouns divided? Define them. Are either of these general classes sub-divided? if so, give the sub-divisions and define each.

5. How many, and what are the ways of distinguishing the Masculine from the Feminine gender?

6. Give the general classes of Adjectives, with their sub divisions? Define each.

7. When is "WHAT" a Relative Pronoun? What other parts of speech may it be? Give examples of each.

8. When is "THAT" a Relative Pronoun? What other parts of speech may it be? Give examples of each.

9. What are the properties of Verbs? Define each.

10. How many and what are the Moods.

11. What is Tense? How many Tenses are there? What are they?

12. How many Tenses has each Mood? What are they?

13. Give the signs of the Tenses in all the Moods?

14. Into how many classes are Adverbs divided? What are they? Define each.

15. What is a Conjunction? Into how many classes are Conjunctions divided? Define each.

16. Analyze the following sentence: "The King of Shadows loves a shining mark."

17. Analyze the following sentence: "The glimmering landscape now fades on the sight."

18. Analyze the following sentence: "The stars will then lift up their heads and rejoice."

19. Analyze the following sentence: "Teachers are anxious that their pupils should improve."

20. Analyze the following sentence: "The Lord uplifts his awful hand and chains you to the shore."

Wm. H. Jackson.

1. What is Mathematics? What is Algebra?

2. How many kinds of quantities are employed in Algebra? What are they, and how are they represented?

3. Explain the difference between a Coefficient and an Exponent. What is an Algebraic Expression?

4. What is a Monominal? A Binominal? A Trinominal? A Polynominal?

5. What are Homogeneous Terms? When is a Polynominal homogeneous? What are Similar Terms?

6. What is the Reciprocal of a quantity? Express the Reciprocal of the following quantities: a, abc, a plus b, a—c.

7. Write a Monominal, a Binominal, a Trinominal, a Polynominal of 4 terms, and all of the same degree.

8. What is the Numerical value of the following expression, when a=4, b=3, c=2 and d=1.

$$\frac{15(a+d+b)}{3c^2} - \frac{a-c}{2} + \frac{3}{abd} + a^3b^3c^3d^3.$$

9. From a, substract—b.

10. Multiply a—b by c—d. Give the rules for the Signs in Multiplication.

Wm. H. Jackson.

1. Express MDCCCXLVIII in figures.

2. What is the Greatest Common Divisor? The Least Common Multiple?

3. What is the Greatest Common Divisor of 408, and 740? Of 441, 567 and 126?

4. What is the Least Common Multiple of 4, 6, 9, 14 and 16? Of 3, 4, 8, and 12?

5. What are the Prime Factors of 9,800?

6. A's income is five times B's; B's income is three times C's; C's income is $1,325; what is their entire income, and the income of each?

7. What number multiplied by 3,047 will produce 299,396,341?

8. A merchant bought 51 pieces of velvet, each piece containing 30 yards, at $8 a yard; he sold it so as to gain $5,000; for what did he sell it?

9. What is a Fraction? What is the Numerator? The Denominator? What is an Improper Fraction? A Complex Fraction?

10. Reduce $\frac{1}{2}$ of $\frac{3}{8}$ of $3\frac{3}{4}$ of $6\frac{5}{8}$ to a whole or mixed number.

11. Reduce $\dfrac{\frac{5}{8} \text{ of } \frac{2}{3}-\frac{3}{8}+\frac{3}{4}\times 3\frac{1}{3}}{\frac{2}{3}-\frac{1}{4}+\frac{5}{8}\times\frac{1}{6}\div\frac{2}{3}}$ to a whole or mixed number.

12. From $\frac{3}{8}$ take $\frac{3}{4}$.

13. What is the value of $\dfrac{\dfrac{\frac{5}{8}+\frac{2}{3}\times\frac{3}{4}-\frac{1}{8}}{\frac{2}{3}}}{\dfrac{\frac{5}{8} \text{ of } \frac{7}{8}+\frac{1}{4}}{\frac{1}{4} \text{ of } \frac{1}{2}}}$

14. How long will it take a man to travel 553 miles, provided he travels $3\frac{1}{2}$ miles per hour, and $9\frac{7}{8}$ hours per day?

15. $\frac{3}{4}$ of 144 is $\frac{2}{3}$ of what number? A, B and C together own $342\frac{1}{2}$ acres of land; A owns $17\frac{1}{3}$ acres more than B, and B owns $20\frac{7}{8}$ acres more than C, how much had each?

16. How many bushels of coal would a box contain measuring 5 feet long, 3 feet deep and 4 feet high? How many tons would the same box contain?

17. What would be the cost of plastering a room 25 feet long, 14 feet wide and 10 feet high, @ 15c. per square yard, allowing for 4 windows, each 3x4 feet, and 1 door 7x3 feet 6 inches?

18. If 59 casks contain 44 hhd. 53 gal. 2 qt. 1 pt. of wine, what is the contents of one-fifth of a cask.

19. A steamship in crossing the Atlantic Ocean has a distance of 3,500 miles to go; if she sails 211 m. 4 fur. 32 rd. a day, what distance has she yet to sail after 15 days.

20. A printer uses 1 sheet of paper for every 16 pages of an octavo book; how much paper will be necessary to print 500 copies of a book containing 336 pages, allowing 2 quires of waste paper in each ream.

LATIN—THIRD FORM.

Prof. R. T. Greener.

Translate:

1. Hoc facinus rex miratur.
2. Pacem te poscimus,
3. Dionysius navigabat Syracusas.
4. Hannibal femur ictus cecidit.
5. Milites non mulieribus, non infantibus pepercerunt.
6. Tu virtutem pracfer divitiis.

7. Trojæ huic loco nomen est.

8. Ego spem pretio non emo.

9. Solis occasu suas copias Ariovistus in castra reduxit.

10. Scipione duce, ponte facto, superaverunt Ticinum flumen.

11. Si te rogavero aliquid, non respondebis ?

12. Philosophia nos docuit, ut nosmet ipsos nosceremus.

13. Equidem vellem, ut redires.

14. Ne quis, tanquam parva, fastidiat grammaticæ elementa.

15. Timoleon oravit omnes, ne id facerent.

16. Lex brevis est, quo facilius ab imperitis teneatur.

17. Oderint, dum metuant.   Licet ipsa vitium sib.

18. Quam magnum vectigal sit parsimonia!

19. Quid est, cur non orator de rebus iis eloquentissime dicat, quas cognorit?

20. In Hortensio memoria tanta fuit, ut, quæ secum commentatus esset, ea verbis iisdem redderet, quibus cogitavisset.

21. Divico ita cum Cæsare egit, si pacem populus Romanus cum Helvetiis faceret, in eam partem ituros Helvetios, ubi eos Cæsar esse voluisset; sin bello persequi persevararet, remiuisceretur pristinæ virtutis Helvetiorum.

22. Cura, ut quam primum venias.

23. Cato esse quam videri doctus malebat.

24. Consul placandis diis dat operam.

25. Pacem petitum legatum Romam mittunt.

26. Dionysius Corinthi expulsus Syracusis pueros docebat.

27. Jus sua sponte est expetendum.

PHYSICAL GEOGRAPHY—PREPARATORY SCHOOL.

Professor H. J. Fox.

1. Name the great circles.

2. Name the zones and give their latitudes.

3. Give the form and measurements of the earth.

4. How do you prove that it is a sphere ?

5. In which Hemisphere is there the most land ?

6. Where is the center of the water on the earth ?

7. Where is the center of the land ?

8. What is the earth's axis ?

9. In what order were its parts created ?

10. What is Physical Geography ?

HISTORY—THIRD FORM.

Prof. H. J. Fox.

1. What is History?
2. To what division of the human race do we belong?
3. What was the ancient language of India?
4. Who divided Europe and Asia with the Aryans?
5. What were the three great divisions of the Semitic nations?
6. How did they disperse?
7. Who were the Celts, and where did they settle?
8. Teutons? and Slaves?
9. What great battles did the Greeks fight? Who were the Generals and Historians?
10. What city became mistress of the world, and how?

SPELLING—PREPARATORY SCHOOL.

Wm. H. Jackson.

Correct the spelling of the following words :

   1. Laybor.
   2. Honney.
   3. Posession.
   4. Colection.
   5. Unmersiful.
   6. Agreing.
   7. Rogueish.
   8. Lyeing.
   9. Guaranteeing.
   10. Changeable.
   11. Morgage.
   12. Unwommanly.
   13. Machinest.
   14. Meriment.
   15. Bridal.
   16. Luxureous.
   17. Poettess.
   18. Sizable.
   19. Deserveing.
   20. Marriagable.

What are the three rules for spelling words ending with " e ?"

GRAMMAR—SECOND FORM.

Wm. H. Jackson.

1. What is language? How many kinds of language, and what are they?

2. What is the distinction between General Grammar and English Grammar? Into how many parts is English Grammar divided? Define each.

3. Give the rules for the use of Capital letters?

4. How many, and what are the parts of Speech? Define each.

5. Into how many classes are Nouns divided? Define them. Are either of these general classes sub-divided, if so, give the sub-divisions and define each.

6. What properties have Nouns? Define each.

7. How many, and what are the ways of distinguishing the Masculine from the Feminine gender?

8. What is Case? How many Cases are there? Define each.

9. How is the Possessive Case Singular found? Plural?

10. In how many ways may Nouns be in the Absolute Case? Give an example of each. When is a Noun in apposition? Give an example.

11. Give the general classes of Adjectives with their sub-divisions. Define each.

12. What is Comparison? How many degrees of Comparison are there? Define each.

13. When is " WHAT " a Relative Pronoun? What other parts of speech may it be? Give examples of each.

14. When is "THAT" a Relative Pronoun? What other parts of speech may it be? Give examples of each.

15. What is the difference between a Transitive and an Intransitive Verb? With respect to their nature into how many classes may Verbs be divided?

16. What are the properties of Verbs? Define each.

17. How many and what are the Moods?

18. What is Tense? How many Tenses are there? What are they?

19. How many Tenses has each Mood? What are they?

20. Give the signs of the Tenses in all the Moods?

Wm. H. Jackson.

1. What is Arithmetic?

2. What is the difference between the Roman and the Arabic Notation?

3. What is the Divisor? The Multiplicand? The Minuend?

4. Express MDCCCXLVIII in figures.

5. Add together "Ten million and ten." "One hundred and five billion, one hundred thousand and seven." "One hundred and one."
"One million and one." Three hundred thousand three hundred."

6. What is the Greatest Common Divisor? The Least Common Multiple?

7. What is the Greatest Common Divisor of 408 and 740? Of 441,
567 and 126?

8. What is the Least Common Multiple of 4, 6, 9, 14 and 16? Of 3,
4, 8 and 12?

9. What are the Prime Factors of 9,800?

10. A's income is five times B's; B's income is three times C's; C's
income is $1,325; what is their entire income, and the income of each?

11. What number multiplied by 3,047 will produce 297,396,341?

12. A merchant bought 51 pieces of velvet, each piece containing 30
yards, at $8 a yard; he sold it so as to gain $5,000; for what did he
sell it?

13. What is the quotient of the product of 10, 6, 84 and 42, divided
by the product of 12, 5, 24, 7?

14. What is a Fraction? What is the Numerator? The Denominator? What is an Improper Fraction? A Complex Fraction?

15. Reduce $\frac{1}{2}$ of $\frac{3}{4}$ of $3\frac{4}{7}$ of $6\frac{5}{8}$ to a whole or mixed number?

16. Reduce $\dfrac{\frac{5}{8} \text{ of } \frac{2}{3} - \frac{3}{4} + \frac{3}{4} \times 3\frac{1}{4}}{\frac{3}{4} - \frac{1}{4} + \frac{5}{9} \times \frac{1}{8} \div \frac{2}{3}}$ to a whole or mixed number.

17. From $\frac{3}{4}$ take $\frac{3}{4}$.

18. What is the value of $\dfrac{\dfrac{\frac{5}{8} + \frac{2}{3} \times \frac{3}{4} - \frac{1}{3}}{\frac{2}{3}}}{\dfrac{\frac{5}{8} \text{ of } \frac{3}{4} + \frac{1}{4}}{\frac{1}{4} \text{ of } \frac{1}{2}}}$

19. How long will it take a man to travel 553 miles, provided he
travels $3\frac{1}{2}$ miles per hour, and $9\frac{1}{5}$ hours per day?

20. $\frac{3}{4}$ of 144 is $\frac{2}{3}$ of what number? A, B and C together own $342\frac{1}{2}$
acres of land; A owns $17\frac{1}{4}$ acres more than B, and B owns $20\frac{1}{4}$ acres
more than C, how much land had each?

GEOGRAPHY—SECOND AND THIRD FORM.

Wm. H. Jackson.

1. What is the distinction between Physical and Political Geography ?
2. What is Longitude? Latitude? What is a Meridian ?
3. Which Hemisphere is the larger ? Which Continent?
4. Name the rivers of Africa. Of Asia.
5. Name the mountains of South America. Of Africa.
6. What are the political divisions of North America ?
7. Bound North America.
8. Describe the Mississippi River. Red. Colorado. Severn. Columbia.
9. Bound New York and give its Capital. Indiana. South Carolina. Maine. Georgia.
10. In sailing from Portland to New Orleans, what Capes, Bays and Coast Cities would you pass ?
11. Name the great Lakes, and state where they are situated.
12. Bound the United States, and give its Capital.
13. Mention all the rivers that flow into the Mississippi.
14. Name the Capital of each State and Territory, and give its location.
15. Name the political divisions of South America. Bound Brazil, Ecuador, Chili, Patagonia, and give the Capital of each, with its location.
16. Which of the South American States is the smallest ? Which the largest ? Give the size of each, as compared with some of the United States.
17. Name some of the volcanoes in South America, and give their location.
18. Bound Mexico. Name its Capital and give its location.
19. Name the Capes and Bays on the Atlantic Coast of the United States, beginning with Maine.
20. Name the principal cities of Canada, and their location.

HISTORY—SECOND FORM.

Wm. H. Jackson.

1. From what Continent did the first inhabitants of America probably come ?
2. What reason is there for supposing that this country was inhabited before its discovery by Columbus ?
3. Give a short history of the Mound Builders; whence they came; their civilization ; and by whom they were succeeded.

4. What is known of the character, disposition and industry of the Indians?

5. Who were the Northmen, and what part do they claim to have taken in the early settlement of America?

6. What was the general idea throughout Europe in the Fifteenth Century, as regards the shape of the Earth?

7. How did Columbus propose to reach the East Indies; was it by the usual route? What was the usual route?

8. After whom was America named? Why was it so named?

9. What four European nations were engaged in the early explorations of America, and what portion or portions of the Continent did each explore?

10. Name the most noted Spanish explorers? Who first circumnavigated the Globe? Name the most noted French explorers? The most noted explorers of other nations?

11. When and by whom was the Pacific Ocean discovered? The Mississippi River?

12. Name the two oldest towns in the United States? When and by whom were they founded?

13. Name the permanent settlements made at the beginning af the seventeenth century?

14. What important event took place in 1492? In 1602? In 1609? In 1620?

15. Give a short account of the settlement of Virginia? What can you say of John Smith?

16. Give an account of the settlement of Massachusetts? What can you say of Roger Williams?

17. Who first settled New York? What name was given it? When and under what circumstances was its name changed?

18. Who was William Penn, and what can you say of his colony?

19. Who settled Maryland, and what can you say of him?

20. What can you say of the settlement of South Carolina, when, and by whom was it first settled?

ARITHMETIC—FIRST FORM.

Harry A. Fox.

1. What is Arithmetic?

2. What is the difference between the Roman and the Arabic Notation?

3. What is Addition? Multiplication? Division?

4. What is the Divisor? The Multiplicand? The Minuend?

5. Express MDCCCXLVIII in figures?

6. What is the value of the expression, $10 \times 8 \div 6 + 105 - 9 \times 9 \div 81$?

7. Add together "Ten million and ten." "One hundred and five billion, one hundred thousand and seven." "One hundred and one." "One million and one." "Three hundred thousand, three hundred."

8. From 97,601 take 99,003.

9. Multiply 9,000,009 by 80,079.

10. Divide 397,664,976 by 308.

11. What is a Prime Factor? A Prime Number?

12. What is the Greatest Common Divisor? The Least Common Multiple?

13. What is the Greatest Common Divisor of 408 and 740? Of 441, 567 and 126?

14. What is the Least Common Multiple of 4, 6, 9, 14 and 16? Of 3, 4, 8 and 12?

15. What are the Prime Factors of 9,800?

16. A's income is five times B's; B's income is three times C's; C's income is $1,325; what is their entire income, and the income of each?

17. A gentleman possessed an estate of $70,288; he gave one-fourth of it to his wife, and divided the remainder equally among his four children. How much did each child receive?

18. What number multiplied by 3,047 will produce 297,396,341?

19. A merchant bought 51 pieces of velvet, each containing 30 yards, at $8 a yard; he sold it so as to gain $5,000; for what did he sell it?

20. What is the quotient of the product of 10, 6, 84 and 42, divided by the product of 12, 5, 24, 7?

GEOGRAPHY—FIRST FORM.

Harry A. Fox.

1. What is Geography?

2. What is the distinction between Physical and Political Geography?

3. What is Longitude? Latitude? What is a Meridian?

4. What is a Continent? An Island? A Cape? A Strait?

5. Which Hemisphere is the larger? Which Continent?

6. What countries compose the Eastern Continent? The Western?

7. Bound Europe. Africa.

8. Name the rivers of Africa. Of Asia.

9. Name the mountains of South America. Of Africa.

10. Where is the Bay of Bengal? Gulf of Guinea? Caspian Sea?

11. What are the political divisions of North America?

12. Bound North America.

13. Where is the Gulf of St. Lawrence? Gulf of Mexico? Baffins' Bay? James' Bay? Bay of Campeachy?

14. Where is Davis' Strait? Banks' Strait? What waters do they connect?

15. Describe the Mississippi River. Red. Colorado. Severn. Columbia.

16. Bound New York and give its Capital. Indiana. South Carolina. Maine. Georgia.

17. In sailing from Portland to New Orleans, what Capes, Bays and Coast Cities would you pass?

18. Name the Great Lakes, and state where they are situated.

19. Bound the United States, and give its Capital.

20. Mention all the rivers that flow into the Mississippi.

HISTORY—FIRST FORM.

Harry A. Fox.

1. From what continent did the first inhabitants of America probably come?

2. What reason is there for supposing that this country was inhabited before its discovery by Columbus?

3. Give a short history of the Mound Builders; whence they came; their civilization; and by whom they were succeeded.

4. What is known of the character, disposition and industry of the Indians?

5. Who were the Northmen, and what part do they claim to have taken in the early settlement of America?

6. What was the general idea throughout Europe in the Fifteenth Century, as regards the shape of the earth?

7. How did Columbus propose to reach the East Indies; was it by the usual route? What was the usual route?

8. Give a short history of the life and discoveries of Columbus?

9. After whom was America named? Why was it so named?

10. Give an account of the discoveries of the Cabots?

11. What four European nations were engaged in the early explorations of America, and what portion or portions of the continent did each explore?

12. Name the most noted Spanish explorers? Who first circumnavigated the Globe?

13. Name the most noted French explorers? The most noted explorers of other nations?

14. When and by whom was the Pacific Ocean discovered? The Mississippi River?

15. Give a short history of the discovery of Florida?

16. Name the two oldest towns in the United States? When and by whom were they founded?

17. Give some account of Sir Walter Raleigh?

18. Give an account of the Dutch settlements in America?

19. Name the permanent settlements made at the beginning of the Seventeenth Century?

20. What important event took place in 1492? In 1602? In 1609? In 1620?

GRAMMAR—FIRST FORM.

Harry A. Fox.

1. What is the difference between spoken and written Language?

2. What is English Grammar?

3. Define the four parts of Grammar.

4. What is an Elementary Sound?

5. What is a Syllable?

6. What is a Vowel? A Consonant? How are Consonants divided?

7. What is a Dipthong? A Digraph? A Trigraph? Give a word containing a Dipthong. One containing a Digraph? One containing a Trigraph.

8. What is a Double Consonant? Give an illustration.

9. Place capital letters where they belong in the following sentence: "on the tenth of january last, i visited the house of representatives, then in session in the city of columbia, south carolina."

10. What is a Derivative Word? A Radical Word?

11. What is a Noun? A Verb? A Participle? An Adjective? An Adverb?

12. How many kinds of Nouns? How many kinds of Common Nouns? Define and give an illustration of each.

13. What is Person? How many kinds of Person are there? Define each.

14. What is Gender? How many kinds of Gender are there? Define each.

15. Give the different ways of distinguishing the Masculine from the Feminine Gender?

16. What is Number? How many Numbers are there? Define each.

17. What are the two rules for the formation of the plural, when the Noun ends in "o"? when it ends in "s"? When it ends in "f"? or "fe"?

18. What is Case? Define the different Cases.

19. What are the rules for forming the Possessive Case, singular and plural? What is the rule when the Noun is a Compound Word?

20. Give a sentence containing a Noun in the Nominative Case. In the Possessive Case. In the Absolute Case. When is a Noun in Opposition? Give an illustration.